THE
OTHER SIDE OF THE BED

What Patients Go Through
and What Doctors Can Learn

Daniel S. Mishkin, M.D.

Copyright © 2017 by Daniel S. Mishkin
All rights reserved.

No part of this book may be reproduced in any form, except for the purpose of reviews, without written permission of the publisher.

Library of Congress Control Number: 2017947013

Paperback: 978-0-692-91237-9

Book design by Michelle Manley

TABLE OF CONTENTS

	Foreword	X
	Introduction	X
1	The Heart in the Palm of My Hand	X
2	Differentials and Denial: Making Diagnostic Decisions	X
3	My Brother's Keeper: Jumping through Hoops in the Oncology Ward	X
4	Hierarchy in Medicine	X
5	It Takes a Village	X
6	What Does Remission Really Mean?	X
7	Not Again: Dealing with Relapse	X
8	An Immense Emotional Toll	X
9	A Delicate Balance: Why We'll Never Get It All Right	X
10	Facing Death with Dignity: It Is Possible	X
11	After the Catastrophe: Moving Forward	X
	Acknowledgments	X

**I dedicate this book to Jason,
Barry's greatest accomplishment.**

FOREWORD

Few times in one's life does one get to meet a person who will forever change him. In my case, Barry Mishkin was one of those people. I was fortunate to have met Barry when he was an intern at Montefiore Medical Center, the hospital in which I've spent my entire career. At the time, I was the associate director of gastroenterology. I played an important role in interacting with all the medical students and house staff who thought they wanted a career in gastroenterology.

What was immediately impressive about Barry was his smile and apparent lightness of being. He always tried to see the positive, in a person or in a difficult situation, and he did so in a way that seemed genuine. He was the consummate optimist, and his optimism was contagious. People were always nicer when they were interacting with him; he truly brought out the best in everyone. I was thrilled that Barry's excellence was recognized by the department, which had the good sense to appoint him chief resident, and I was devastated when he was diagnosed with acute lymphocytic leukemia just before beginning his GI fellowship. Although he missed much of the fellowship, if his white blood cell count, hemoglobin level, and energy stores

Daniel S. Mishkin, M.D.

allowed it, he would appear on scene and try to participate, try to make a go of it, even though his body wanted nothing more than to rest. I remember vividly wrapping my arms around Barry to support him physically while instructing him how to manipulate a gastroscope. Often, mid-procedure, he would say that he was sorry, but he was too weak to continue. On the occasions that the procedure could be completed with only Barry holding the scope, a brighter smile never lit up a room. I learned from him never to take the daily routine for granted, an insight I keep close to my heart today. One is blessed to be able to do the mundane.

Barry's passing left a hole in my heart, but his presence gives me a constant reminder to be the nicest person I can be. Barry's story, as told by his brother Daniel, also a fabulous GI fellow who offers the same nonjudgmental, smiling reminder, is told from a deeply personal place. It is a painful memory laced with strands of joy and laughter that urges the reader to strive always to do his or her best, to see the good in everyone, and to never leave any task or responsibility with an undotted "i" or uncrossed "t." Moreover, it reminds us, the caretakers, to stifle our arrogance and to recognize that sometimes we don't know it all and can learn important lessons from the patient. The precious characteristics that made Barry so very special are now formally recognized in the Barry Mishkin Award, which is given each year by the Department of Medicine at its graduation ceremony to the graduating resident who exhibits "humanity, ethics, and excellence in the practice of medicine," a constant reminder of a practice worth striving for.

Lawrence J. Brandt, MD, MACG, AGAF, FASGE, NYSGEF
Professor of Medicine and Surgery
Albert Einstein College of Medicine
Emeritus Chief, Division of Gastroenterology
Montefiore Medical Center
Bronx, NY 10467

1
THE HEART IN THE PALM OF MY HAND

It was a Thursday afternoon, around 2:30 p.m. I was a second-year internal-medicine resident working in the coronary care unit. The emergency room was relatively quiet and we had finished afternoon rounds. I had already assigned all the admissions for the afternoon. Casually, I said to myself, "I might get out of here early."

As soon as I'd opened my mouth, I regretted it. In the hospital, it's bad luck to say "It looks quiet," or anything to that effect. At the sound of those words, alarms begin to ring. In the hospital, crises always seem to come in waves. There are spurts of relative calm, followed by the utter chaos of simultaneous codes.

Moments later, over the intercom, I heard an announcement: a code in the cardiac catheterization (cath) lab. Codes differ in their severity. A code might be an early warning, a call for additional hands, or an alarm for someone who's lost his heartbeat—a patient who's literally dead. I knew right away that a code in the cardiac cath lab meant real trouble. There had to be at least one cardiologist on-site, as well as skilled nurses trained in

Daniel S. Mishkin, M.D.

cardiac resuscitation. If they couldn't handle the situation, it was serious.

When I arrived in the room, I noticed an overwhelming silence. The only voice I heard was the cardiologist's, calling the shots as he pumped the patient's chest. The patient was in real trouble. For one reason or another, a large bolus of air had been injected into the bloodstream. It was going straight to the heart and brain, and it would likely lead to a terminal event.

There I was, right in the middle of the crisis, standing next to the cath lab table where the lifeless patient lay, right in the middle of the crisis. There were plenty of other people who had recognized the severity of the call and responded to the code. The cardiologist singled out the most senior physicians, residents, and nurses, sending everyone else aside. I was one of the residents he told to stay in the action. I'd been involved in plenty of codes; I work well in the middle of things, doing the hands-on work required to bring patients back from the brink. It's an adrenaline rush. Of course, I would never want to be the patient or his family in that moment, but I've always gotten a thrill out of doing the split-second work that can save a life.

This code in the cath lab was like nothing I had ever seen before. We knew that we had to think outside of the box. The cardiologist suggested that we place a needle directly into the patient's heart and drain out the air. It was like I'd been dropped into a TV medical drama, but with a real patient in front of me. I saw the needle pierce the skin and go right to where the heart is, then saw the syringe pull back air. It was outrageous!

Despite the cardiologist's impressive work, the patient was still in trouble. I could see what needed to happen next. I told one person to get a cardiac surgeon and another to get a chest saw. We needed to pump the heart muscle manually, as shocking alone would not do the trick at this time. The cardiologist, who could have yelled at me for issuing orders out

The Other Side of the Bed

of turn, expressed his approval with a quick nod. It was surprising that I knew what was needed: I had never been in this situation before. I wouldn't know what the chest saw looked like if someone had sent me to get it, but I could envision what had to happen. We continued to siphon the air from the heart chamber, repeatedly stabbing the patient with the large needle. Then, the cardiac surgeon rushed in. With a calm tone and a few words, he took charge.

He grabbed a bottle of iodine cleaning solution and poured it over the patient's chest. This was nothing like the pre-op prep work I'd seen and done before. In medical school, getting to prep patients for surgery was like a carrot for me. If I stayed late post-call, completed all my notes, and sucked up to the attending, the senior physician in charge, and the chief resident, I would be allowed to prep the patient's skin before surgery. In the operating room, I would do the painstaking work of sterilizing the patient's skin before cutting. I was taught to carefully spread the iodine cleaning solution and meticulously clean from the inside outward in a slow, systematic approach. In the cath lab code situation, there was no time for a ten-minute sterilization process.

Just at the last moment, a nurse came rushing through the door with the chest saw. The cardiac surgeon grabbed it and cracked the patient's chest open in less than ten seconds. Upon gaining access to the heart cavity, we found this precious organ lying still. It wasn't beating.

The surgeon began squeezing the heart, and when he needed to do something else, he told me to grab the patient's heart and start pumping. It felt like I was in a MASH unit in a combat zone. I did as he said; the feeling was indescribable. I had dissected a heart in anatomy lab, but it felt nothing like this heart which, just minutes before, was beating on its own. Now, the heart was in the palm of my hand. The surgeon grabbed the paddles, called

Daniel S. Mishkin, M.D.

"Clear!" and tried to shock the heart back into rhythm, without success. Then, his voice still calm and clear, the surgeon told me to start pumping again. We moved the patient to the stretcher and the surgeon climbed onto the bed, straddled the patient, and began pumping the heart himself. With the assistance of a security officer, the other staff cleared the way for a direct path to the elevator and into the operating room.

My job was done. The patient was in the hands of the person who needed to take care of him, but my thoughts were still racing. I was on a real high—with the cardiologist's quick thinking and the surgeon's skill, we opened up the patient and gave him a fighting chance in an otherwise fatal situation. Delays, even on the order of seconds, could have yielded devastating results.

After the patient had been wheeled away, the silence was deafening. I realized that in a blink of an eye, twenty minutes had passed. I started to realize what had been accomplished. It had been an eternity for the patient. I looked around. There was blood everywhere. My gown, goggles, and gloves were all slicked with red blood, just like everyone else's. We were all afraid to speak. We'd likely just saved a patient's life, but there was no celebrating. I wanted to scream and jump to let out the adrenaline, but you just can't. No matter how much you want to celebrate, it's not appropriate, not professional. I knew that. The patient's family was just outside the door, hanging on to our every movement and word. How would it have looked if we had high-fived or smiled? Doctors do not have to be wrong in their actions to be perceived as being inappropriate.

The doctors, nurses, and assistants in the room were all in shock. After a few minutes, we began to debrief, discussing what had happened and recognizing the positives and negatives of the event. We needed to learn from this experience for future patient care. A lot of what happens in a code, just like other aspects of medicine, needs to be instinctual, but there's always something to learn from each case. If you discuss it shortly after it happens, you can sift out those nuggets of wisdom. We also had to reset and ground ourselves again; we had to get back to work.

I strongly believe that as physicians, we do not decide who lives or dies. Rather, we are messengers at the hands of a higher power. We are very lucky to be given the opportunity to participate in the care of others. We see people at their worst of times and try to help them. At the end of the day, though, we have to go home and live with our experiences and our mistakes. It's a hard thing for anyone outside our profession to grasp. Being a physician is a cross between being a member of a military group and a fraternity: We generally understand where someone else is coming from because he or she went through the same training and system. We might laugh together to blow off steam from a stressful situation, while others looking on might see that laughter as inappropriate. Context matters.

I'm so lucky to have come from a medical family. My father and brother both preceded me into the field of gastroenterology, and they taught me the values that guide me still to this day. My father was always a role model, and my brother was my best friend. Even though my brother Barry passed away more than fourteen years ago, my admiration for him has never diminished, and in many ways, it still drives me. I continue to push myself to live up to his example. Since Barry's death, I've tried to live with the tenacious spirit and generous heart I learned from his life, illness, and death.

Growing up, I idolized my brother. Barry was six years old when I was born, so of course I saw him through a younger brother's rose-colored glasses. As soon as I could walk, I followed him everywhere. If he was watching TV, I was watching *him* (a scene I've eerily seen my three daughters repeat with me). The amazing thing about Barry, though, was that he didn't just brush off the attention. He included me. Most teenagers wouldn't let a nine-year-old tag along, but he did. We were always close, always together.

His confidence, magnetism, and self-assured open nature made him a social lion. When he walked into a room, everyone's attention turned to him. He wasn't particularly gregarious, but he always wore a big, goofy smile that put others at ease.

That goofy smile is the biggest similarity Barry and I shared in appearance. I look much more like our mom, and he looked more like our dad. In the summer, with his hair sun-bleached and nearly blond, he was a Nordic ideal. He was always fit, and he loved sports—especially hockey. In the summer, he'd water-ski behind the boat at our parents' lake house, attempting acrobatics he was in no way prepared for, laughing as he tumbled over the water's surface. I still have the videos.

My father was completely devoted to caring for others, both as a physician and a family man. Growing up in the comfort of our father's care, my brother always knew he wanted to be a doctor too. Dad was someone whom our family and community could rely on in a crisis. When Barry, at his first birthday party, got something stuck in his throat, Dad jumped in. He performed the Heimlich maneuver and, with his adrenaline pumping, was ready to pull out a knife and do a tracheotomy. Luckily, though, my mom jumped in to calm him down. "He's breathing," she said. My mom always has a way of stabilizing hectic situations, a perfect counterpart to my father.

Barry had no memory of that episode, but all the party guests remember it. They still tell the story. The medical incident that affected him much more didn't happen until he was twelve. I was five and a half or so. Barry had his tonsils removed, and a few days later, he started to hemorrhage.

I saw him vomit red blood, then saw Dad's arms scoop him up and rush him to the hospital. Once they arrived, the doctors had trouble stabilizing my brother; they could barely even place an IV in him. They ended up having to take Barry into surgery to pack him and stop the bleeding. Years later, he told me, "I was traumatized." Thanks to the doctors' and my father's quick work, however, Barry survived.

Some combination of our father's heroic example and Barry's personal experiences propelled him toward medicine. Many young doctors enter the field because they're naturally good at science and math. For Barry, the academic side was at times a struggle. He loved science, though, and he was a very hard worker. He was never the top student, but he dreamed of going to medical school. Focused on this singular goal, Barry attacked each step methodically. He studied for the MCAT®, pushed hard on his scholastic exams, and padded his CV with research and extracurricular activities.

When Barry was accepted to Albert Einstein College of Medicine in the Bronx, a whole new world opened up to him. A sheltered young man from the quiet streets of Côte Saint-Luc, Montreal, was now in the big city and in pursuit of his dreams. The poverty and diversity in the Bronx were like nothing Barry had ever seen. When Barry first got to the program, his colleagues told him stories of frequent burglaries and con men in the parking lot, as well as about the various pockets of organized crime. The neighborhood was controlled by ethnic mafias, each of which held sway in a different arena. It was 1991, in the thick of the crack epidemic, years before Rudy Giuliani became mayor and cleaned up the city. There Barry was.

He quickly learned how to act. By the time I visited, a couple of months after he'd moved, he knew the rules. As we drove down the street, he told me, "Never honk at anyone here. People carry weapons."

Daniel S. Mishkin, M.D.

We were driving to Manhattan to see the sights. I was seventeen, eager to see my older brother and his new home. My mom had sent me down to visit with a suitcase packed full of homemade food, perfectly portioned so he'd have meals for a month. I was excited to be there and see his new life, and also to bring him a little taste of home.

We parked the car on the Upper West Side and took the subway downtown. On the train, I was thrilled. Then, at one end of the car, a group of people started to move. They were coming toward the middle of the car—toward *us*. At the other end, another group, also moving toward us and looking at the first group. They were about to fight.

"We have to get off this train," Barry said, and as soon as the train stopped, we jumped off. From the platform, we watched the two groups converge. They started to pummel each other, in the middle of the subway car, right where we'd just been standing seconds before. I was breathing hard, terrified, but Barry put his hand on my shoulder and said, "Just calm down; it is OK. Relax." He was always able to calm me down.

I knew he was afraid too. In unpredictable situations, he kept his cool. Later, if he called my parents, he'd break down. He was mentally tough in some situations and openly emotional in others. But in the heat of the moment, you could count on him.

Thanks in part to its location in the Bronx, Einstein was a great place to study medicine. The patients, doctors, and staff there came from all walks of life and many different countries; he got to experience medicine in a truly global context. He treated immigrants with rare diseases and gunshot victims from around the block. He loved meeting new people, experiencing a new environment, and learning how to save lives. He was openly curious, like a child. He often said to me, "I'll never grow up. That will be my key to success."

As a part of his first year of medical school, Barry was offered the chance to further his education by following a patient with a chronic illness or working in a more challenging environment, a weekly clinic at the New York City jail at Rikers Island. Rikers, located just beyond LaGuardia Airport, is where people are taken after they're arrested. They can be held there for trial or to serve sentences of up to a year. It's a melting pot of all kinds of criminals. There's little stability, plenty of gang activity, and limited access to health care. Those factors made it exactly the place where Barry knew he had to go. He wanted to go where he was most needed.

In the beginning of medical school, it's rare to feel needed. Mostly, you feel as if you're in the way. You don't really know anything yet, so it's hard to *feel* productive. For Barry, Rikers was a place where he could do so much just by showing up. Our dad always told us the key to life was often "Just show up." It was his way of telling us to get the experience so that we'd develop the skills we needed to care for patients. Of course, my parents worried every time Barry went to Rikers. Barry was a good son though. He'd call our parents once he got back and tell them, "It's OK; I'm back. I didn't get kidnapped or killed."

Mom was shocked when he first told her about the opportunity. She wanted to talk him out of it. Dad was nervous, but he understood. In medical education, there's a general consensus that the best young doctors get their training in the most difficult environments. The more you see, the more you practice, and the more you practice, the more chance you have to learn from witnessing extreme situations.

My dad's personal experience supported that consensus. He was in Baltimore studying medicine at Johns Hopkins in 1968. On the day of Dr. Martin Luther King Jr.'s assassination, the city exploded in riots. People threatened to attack the hospital and the doctors. My dad, his supervisors, and the rest of the hospital kept working. Security guards had to surround the hospital buildings. Patients made threats against my dad, and for his own safety, he kept a list of everyone whom he'd cared for who had then gone to prison. That experience taught my father to make tough decisions under pressure, an experience that he believed shaped him as a doctor. Working under tough conditions sharpens your reflexes. He had understood why Barry wanted to take on the challenge of Rikers, and therefore, he'd supported his son's decision.

At Rikers, my clean-cut brother found himself treating hardened criminals. The clinic was a world away from the modern hospital where he would eventually work. He loved the work he did there. The medical officers were enthusiastic about teaching. They knew the students who chose to rotate through there were motivated. They played a lot of "radiology rounds"—looking at films from past cases and making hypotheses. Often, inmates involved in conflicts inside the facility would try to get away for a few days by swallowing things; the clinic was their Club Med, a place to get away from their reality. The most common things to swallow, and thus get you off your cell block, were razor blades wrapped in cellophane tape. They wrapped the blade in tape to limit the damage, but if the doctors couldn't see the tape on the X-rays, they would have to send the inmates to the hospital in the city, outside of Rikers. In transit, there could be the opportunity for the inmate to meet up with people on the outside, or even escape. At the very least, they got to spend a few days out of their cell.

One afternoon, during Barry's normal clinic hours, a group of guards rushed in carrying a prisoner with blood dripping down his chest and all over his lower body. Nobody could tell where the blood was coming from because the man was writhing and screaming in the guards' arms. After a struggle, they restrained him on a gurney. Finally, a medical officer was able to get close enough to see where the bleeding was coming from. The officer looked down and traced the blood streams back to the man's chest; he had a huge hole gouged out of his left chest muscle. Everyone in the clinic jumped in to help pack the wound and stop the bleeding. There were cries of "How did this happen?!" and "What's going on?!"

Just a few moments later, the answer came. Another inmate entered the clinic, escorted by half a dozen correctional officers. In his mouth was a piece of flesh: the chunk of chest muscle torn from the first bleeding man.

There, in front of the entire clinic staff, surrounded by guards, were two men who had just engaged in a violent altercation. It was the doctors' job to care for their wounds. Once the two inmates were sedated, Barry was assigned to stitch up the second man who came in, the one who had torn out a piece of another man's flesh with his teeth. Both had been injured in the altercation.

I think Barry got an adrenaline rush from working in a crisis like that, but later in the year he started to have second thoughts. Barry learned to expect the unexpected at Rikers. He also learned to be careful. He worried about contracting hepatitis because it was rampant there, and at the time, there weren't any good treatments for it. There were plenty of other problems that could arise from being in the wrong place at the wrong time. He saw a lot of aches and bruises, injuries from fights, and self-harm. He kept a smile on his face, but he worried about his safety. He began to think of Rikers as a rite of passage rather than a thrill. Maybe he even grew up a little.

Barry's manner of enthusiastically running into the toughest environment was something I admired. When I was in my first year of medical school, there were no programmatic options, and I was only able to work on a longitudinal single-patient assessment with a diabetic patient. I accompanied her to medical appointments and thus learned about treating

Daniel S. Mishkin, M.D.

chronic disease from the patient's perspective. While it was much less exotic than Barry's rotation at Rikers, I knew it was important to build a wide range of experiences. I'd watched my brother take on tough cases and make the most of crazy situations, and I'd grown up with my father's stories, so I knew that there is more to medicine than just studying. There is a world of people who need care and many ways doctors need to give it.

In Canada, the whole medical system is structured differently from the way it is in the United States. In the United States, an intern would never be left to tend to the intensive care unit by himself, but one night in Montreal, I found myself doing just that. I had no on-site supervision, just whoever was on call ten or fifteen minutes away. Suddenly, one patient's heartbeat dropped to a dangerous level, too slow to pump blood throughout the body. I slapped on a transcutaneous pacemaker, specialized pads that can be used to electrically shock the heart through the skin, to force it to keep pace with the body's needs. It didn't work. The nurses were right at my side, telling me exactly what to do and getting the attending on the phone. I heard him say through the receiver, "Put in the transvenous pacers if the transcutaneous pacers don't work; I'll be there in ten minutes." I remember thinking, *This is insane. Someone needs to call a doctor. How could* I *do* that?

I had tried to use the transcutaneous pacer without success. Now, I had to try to float a transvenous pacemaker in, to shock the patient's heart directly. I'd never done it; I'd never even seen anyone else do it. This was definitely above my level. I knew it was the only way, so I started to prep for it. The nurses guided me along as I readied myself to put a line into the patient's neck and gain the access to put the transvenous pacer into his heart. Fortunately, the attending arrived just as I had essentially prepped everything and I watched as he skillfully placed the catheter into the heart to control the pacing. It was amazing to watch. The intervention was handled quickly. The patient ended up doing well, and had a permanent pacemaker placed the next day.

Six months later, the exact same thing happened again. I was still an intern, and at two or three in the morning, I was preparing to float a transvenous pacer. In an American hospital, only a cardiology fellow would be able to do that. I was under supervision, but this time I was running the situation and not just relying on the nurses. First, I had tried the transcutaneous pacers. They didn't work. I had started the central access for the transvenous pacer and was getting ready to feed it in when the cardiologist came in and took over. Such an experience made me better equipped for the next instance. Because I'd gone through the motions before, I knew what the steps were and how to proceed. I loved jumping into a crisis situation and doing my part in the everyday work of medicine. The more motivated I was and the more I was willing to work, the more the physicians and nurses would teach me and let me participate. From the first day of my internship, I was getting incredible experience, experience that would sharpen my reflexes and improve my technical acumen. It wasn't quite Barry Mishkin at Rikers, but it was important nonetheless.

2
DIFFERENTIALS AND DENIAL

Making Diagnostic Decisions

Then things changed. In 1999 I was an intern at McGill University and Barry was chief resident for internal medicine at Montefiore Medical Center, the University Hospital for Albert Einstein College of Medicine. We were separated by six years in age and three hundred miles in distance, but we talked almost daily. On Wednesday, March 17, I finished morning rounds and saw that I had a message from Barry. Since we talked all the time, I didn't make much of it. Speaking during the day wasn't unusual for us. He'd call me sometimes to consult on cases, or to see if there was something he could add to my differentials.

We had seen each other days before, when he and his wife Sari brought their newborn son Jason to meet the family in Montreal. In those early, emotional days of fatherhood, Barry was on edge. Now that I'm a father, I know there's something about your firstborn that's so confusing, all-consuming, and chaotic. Barry was working as chief resident, spending as much time with his child as possible, and trying to help his wife recover from pregnancy and birth. He wasn't getting much sleep, so his normal anxiety was kicked up almost to a level of paranoia.

Barry was entering a new phase in his life, and he had been overcome with concern about making sure his family was taken care of. That weekend, my father, my brother, and I, the three Drs. Mishkin, had made a pact to watch over each other and our extended families. Who would have known how quickly we would have to put this into practice?

Physicians can be the worst patients. We have a hard time seeing ourselves on the other side of the bed. We're so focused on treating others, we imagine that we're invincible.

I remember a gifted gastroenterologist in Montreal who exemplified this terrible problem. This physician was experiencing clear symptoms that would suggest advanced colon cancer. However, he delayed a diagnostic colonoscopy for a month because he did not want to disrupt or ruin his daughter's upcoming wedding. He was trying to be selfless, but it ended up costing him his life. The doctor began his chemo treatment later than optimally desired; his cancer was far too advanced. When he finally did begin to receive chemotherapy, it devastated his immune system. He was trying to work through treatment when he picked up a minor infection—a fever. He didn't realize, when he took his temperature, that he was suffering from febrile neutropenia, a condition that results when one's white blood cells are entirely gone.

As per the protocol for febrile neutropenia, the gastroenterologist had to be admitted for IV antibiotics. Yet while he was being admitted, he began barking orders, attempting to take charge to try and improve his odds— it was heartbreaking because he was able to foresee his coming death. Shockingly, he succumbed to his illness later that night.

When I saw Barry's message, I decided to call him back later that day, after midday teaching rounds, when I wasn't as busy. Toward the end of his visit to Montreal, Barry and I had a rare argument. It wasn't quite resolved by the time he departed, so I wanted to give us plenty of time to talk. I didn't think it would be a big deal. I had no idea that our lives were about to be turned upside-down. Even with my years of medical school and training, nothing could have prepared me for what my family was about to go through.

I continued working until I got a call from my sister Sharon.

"You have to call Barry," she said. "He thinks he's dying."

Ridiculous, I thought. I know that, so far, I've presented my brother as nearly perfect, but he was extremely human when it came to the way he thought about himself and our family. Like the rest of us, he could be fearful, sometimes to an extreme. He used to warn me that I could easily be abducted by aliens while driving in the Laurentians, a rural area north of Montreal. He used to propose outlandish diagnoses for every minor ache that afflicted my sister or me. *He's anxious,* I told myself now. *He's on edge. Maybe even a little paranoid with all that stress and so little sleep.* He had a history of falling for conspiracy theories and coming up with hypochondriacal diagnoses for himself, as well as for the rest of the family. This time, things were different. I was told to call him at home, but I didn't expect to find him there. When I heard his voice, my ears started ringing.

"I'm in trouble," he said, his voice low and quivering. He was usually so assertive. So sure of himself. Something was radically different this time. He was home in the middle of the day. He couldn't be in real trouble. Not my big brother. He couldn't be.

"Tell me what's going on," I said.

"I'm in trouble," he said. "Can you come down?"

I could barely breathe.

"Yeah, of course," I said cautiously, "but tell me what's happening."

He paused.

"Since we got back from Montreal, I've been having a hard time."

"What do you mean?" I asked, beginning to feel dizzy.

"I can barely get through rounds. This morning there was blood on my pillow and crust in my nostrils; I think I've been having nosebleeds in my sleep. I started myself on antibiotics a couple of days ago, but I'm getting worse."

"What if you just have a cold? Or an infection? You only took two days off when Jason was born. You could've picked up a virus in the birthing ward."

Barry, normally such a positive person, seemed completely enervated. He didn't have his typical quick responses. We usually jumped over each other to reach differential diagnoses, but this time we were moving much more slowly.

"Listen; this morning my heart rate was over a hundred, so I took my bloods. There are blasts on my smear. It's not good."

"OK, OK, hold on a second."

I wanted time to stop. I knew what blasts on the smear meant. *Leukemia*. It couldn't be. It *couldn't* be.

"Could it be a mistake? Did you rerun the test?"

"One of my mentors, a hematologist, looked at it. I'm admitting myself, it's taken care of, but can you call Mom and Dad? When can you get here?"

When I hung up the phone, I was stunned, completely deflated. The rest of the world kept moving as if nothing had happened, but my older brother, my best friend, was in trouble. Cancer trouble. I couldn't think.

Strangely, I had been thinking about blood cancers a very short time before I talked to Barry. Hematologic malignancies had been the topic of the midday teaching rounds, which all the residents in the internal-medicine department were required to attend. We were given lunch and a break in the middle of our hectic day, and an attending would lead a presentation.

That day, I'd been five minutes late, and the hematologist presenting, Dr. G., decided to pick on me. She was a teacher I respected and a fantastic patient-care advocate, so I didn't mind. I understood the rules of the game; I had to pay my dues. When she picked on me, I knew it was a way of developing my professional relationship with her. I wanted to be challenged and engaged by my teachers. I named characteristics of various leukemias and made accurate assessments in case presentations. Afterward, I felt pretty good; I was proud of myself for having done well on this "pop quiz." I had no idea that I could be so confident in a subject, yet really know nothing about it. I had no clue that later that day, with my brother's health on the line, I would be racing to Dr. G. for advice.

Throughout my life, I've been good with book learning and common sense. Learning medicine was no exception to that. Yet in medicine, you have to apply the book knowledge to radically different individual cases. You have to translate ideal cases to what actually presents. Then you have to learn to treat the person—not just the disease. As an intern, I could recite protocols I'd learned from poring over papers, and I could memorize almost anything, but I was not equipped or expected to treat the whole patient.

After I got off the phone with Barry, I did a quick literature search, trying to find anything but leukemia to explain his symptoms. I found a few studies that showed that, in rare cases, the antibiotic Barry had taken for his symptoms could cause the blood test abnormalities his results showed. I ran to Dr. G., and she dropped everything to counsel me. She was very

Daniel S. Mishkin, M.D.

calming, but she said that the diagnosis would most likely be leukemia. I had to get down to New York as soon as possible. She gave me her home phone number and told me to call. She kept in touch throughout Barry's illness and was an invaluable resource.

Then, I walked into my residency director's office and told him what was happening. He gave me leave to do what I needed to do for my family.

"Drive safely," he said.

It started to hit me. I remembered that Barry had asked me to contact our parents. I called my mom at work, and she and I decided to meet at home. She worked with my dad at his medical practice. My dad happened to be traveling that day, and he couldn't be reached. I was so glad that my mom was there; she has the uncanny ability to remain calm and collected in a crisis. She's extremely methodical. For years, she worked in a lab doing clinical research in gastroenterology with one of my dad's colleagues. When my dad opened up his own practice, she went to work with him as his office manager. She can stay up all night cooking and cleaning before a big family gathering, then go to work the next morning and run the whole show. At this point, with my brother's life on the line, she kept me focused. We packed up and got on the road to New York.

I cut a five-hour drive down to three, arriving around nine-thirty that night. I dropped my mom off at Barry's apartment—she was going to stay there with Jason, to relieve Sari's parents who had been there all day. I continued straight to the hospital.

I had done an elective at Montefiore a year earlier, so I knew my way around. This time, however, it felt different. As doctors we learn to depersonalize illness, but this was so personal. This time, I was no longer a trainee; I was the brother of a cancer patient.

The Other Side of the Bed

I entered the oncology ward at ten o'clock at night to find my brother receiving a transfusion. He had oxygen tubes in his nose. He could barely lift his head. We were still waiting on another round of tests to provide his precise diagnosis. My big brother, my hero, was like Superman surrounded by kryptonite.

We spoke for a minute or two, and he barely stayed awake. I just wanted him to know that I was there, that Mom was with Jason. I wanted him to know that I would stay there at the hospital all night with him and Sari. Barry was a strong guy, but he could also be a mama's boy sometimes. I wanted the family's presence to be a comfort. I also knew he was in agony.

Then, I felt myself start to break down. I grabbed a few of my books and told him I had to study. As soon as I crossed the threshold into the hallway, I collapsed. I was mentally and physically drained, but I was fixated on figuring out how to prove the tests wrong. I spent all night poring over my textbooks.

If you hear hooves, you look for horses, not zebras, right? Well, in medicine, we're taught to avoid missing the rare disease, the zebra. But we also know that common things are common—if you hear hooves, look for horses. And yet, I was desperate to find the uncommon, exotic zebra. What if Barry's symptoms came from a rare medication-related complication? What if it were something else? I've always wanted to be the person who can see the thing that no one else sees. What if the thing I discovered could save my brother?

I was having trouble keeping myself collected. I had rushed to New York from Montreal following a grueling hospital shift to find my brother lying so still in a hospital bed. He couldn't lift his head or arms. When I had entered his room for the first time that night, he'd stretched out his fingers toward me. He was barely strong enough to ask me to hold his hand. I held it in both of my palms and felt myself overcome with emotion, almost in tears. I couldn't let myself cry in front of him.

He was with his wife, and I wanted to let them be alone together. I told them I had to go study. I spent the night in the hallway, on a couch, furiously reading leukemia research. I wasn't absorbing any of the information. I kept reading paragraphs again and again, retaining little to nothing yet still pressing on. That night, I slept on the hallway couch while Barry's wife, Sari, slept in a chair at his bedside, holding his hand. Their fairy-tale world of a strong marriage and beautiful newborn son had just been shattered. They didn't know how this would end.

In the early hours of the next day, reality crept in. Throughout the night, people had come and gone, taking vitals and such, but the morning brought a fresh swarm of friends and colleagues. The other residents were constantly coming in and out of Barry's room. They couldn't believe that one of their own was in the bed. All kinds of people who weren't on Barry's service came in to check on him, offer advice, and try to do something for their valued chief resident who had suddenly become one of their patients.

Denial was fading into the urgent need to act. If it really *was* what we thought it was, there was so much to do. It wasn't just about treatment; it was personal. I wasn't just a doctor anymore; I was a brother.

I couldn't say "cancer"—none of us could—but I *knew* the worst was true. Just a few hours later, a hematologist came in with the words "acute leukemia." The doctor's words made the whole thing very real.

When a doctor gives you news like that, everything but fear fades away. Nothing can be normal again. As we're taught in medical school, there are basic guidelines for giving bad news: Make sure you're in a private place. Give the patient plenty of time to react and ask questions. Never give a cancer diagnosis unless you're completely sure. Beyond that, it's a skill that can only come with experience. It's one of those things in medicine that can't be easily taught.

There are two sides to the patient's bed: that of the physician and that of the patient. As Barry's brother, I was on the patient's side of the bed, backing him up as best I could. Being on the other side of the bed gave me the experience to relate to patients in difficult circumstances. I'm not sure that it's a good thing, but I've been told that I'm good at giving bad news. A patient once told me, "If I have to get bad news, I want to get it from you."

It's not about my personality. I'm not warmer or more empathetic than other physicians. It's less about emotion and more about providing information with clarity and openness.

When patients are referred to me for a procedure or a consultation, they're already nervous. Maybe they have a family history of colon cancer, or they're concerned about symptoms. There's always something weighing on them when they enter my office. Because of their anxieties about their health, I have to overcome any communication barriers before I can diagnose and treat them.

One way I break down those barriers is by asking patients, "What are you afraid of?" It sounds simple, but it's something doctors might skip over, relying on their own assumptions. The fact is, though, you need a patient's full understanding and input in order to treat them properly. Patients come in with a fear or concern, and as doctors, we have to listen in order to address their needs. We can't always assume that we know what's going on. If we're going to help, we have to listen. Sometimes, a little information is worse than no information.

Not long ago, a patient came to see me for a colonoscopy. She was a forty-six-year-old woman, and for the previous year she'd experienced

Daniel S. Mishkin, M.D.

worsening bleeding from her rectum: bright-red blood in her stools. Because her primary-care physician had referred her directly for the procedure, I hadn't met her for an evaluation beforehand.

In my initial interview with her, I found out that she had received in-vitro fertilization treatments, and she believed she might finally be pregnant, as she had missed her period for two months. Given that, we had to check her pregnancy status before we could proceed. I told her we needed to run a pregnancy test, and it would take some time to be sure. She gladly agreed. She was just so hopeful and excited about the possibility of a baby. The test came back negative.

We began the procedure. Just a few seconds in, it was clear that her minimal rectal bleeding was actually from cancer. From what we could evaluate endoscopically, it looked extensive. I really felt for her. I wanted to find the right time and place to tell her.

She was fighting for her life. While I didn't have all the information yet, I knew the odds were stacked against her. This was ten years into my career. I felt confident in what I saw, and I knew I had to tell her. Immediately after the procedure, that's impossible; the patient is waking up from sedation, and there's no way to talk to them in a private area. Hospital curtains are *not* soundproof.

Because I had to wait, though, I was able to make some calls. I wanted to put the next steps in place so that when I did tell her, I'd already have made some arrangements so that she could move ahead toward treatment. She was in for the fight of her life.

It's hard to deal with experiences like that. I had seen a patient at her most hopeful, then at a moment of mortal reckoning. There's a certain level of depersonalization that gets you through the day, but you also have to let yourself relate to others. It's the only way to treat the whole patient.

I once diagnosed a patient, a man who was eighty-one, with gastric cancer. He opted not to have treatment. He told me, "I've lived a good life. I lost my wife seven years ago, and I want to be with her."

He accepted the diagnosis, and he wanted to say his good-byes and live out his time in the manner of his choosing. That doesn't mean he didn't have fears or concerns. From day to day, fears change. Some patients fear losing mental function. Others are afraid they won't be able to make decisions for themselves. The gastric-cancer patient's primary fear was pain.

He asked me, "When I get toward the end and I'm in pain, will I be able to get medication?" He had seen his wife die in pain, and he did not want that.

I said, "Of course you can. Absolutely."

I then knew that if he had a health crisis, pain was one of the first things I needed to check in with him about. He was afraid of being in pain, and because he'd told me, it was my responsibility as his doctor to provide him the necessary relief without extraordinary measures when the time came. Less than a year later, the patient passed at home, surrounded by his loving family. I can only hope he is reunited with his wife now.

One of Barry's initial concerns was simply how to be a patient in the hospital where he worked. He was the chief resident in internal medicine. He'd trained there since medical school. Everybody at Montefiore knew him and everybody liked him. In medical school we are taught to depersonalize patients, but Barry was surrounded by doctors who knew him *personally*. The clear-cut boundaries between physician and patient just didn't apply. A simple X-ray caused a commotion in the hallway.

The first twenty-four hours were full of tests. There were simple tests like X-rays and blood tests; then there was the bone marrow biopsy. The test requires that a hole be drilled into the patient's bone, usually the hip

Daniel S. Mishkin, M.D.

bone, with a large needle. To me, a bone marrow biopsy is one of the most barbaric procedures we perform while a patient is conscious. Barry went through this procedure, only for the aspiration to come out dry. The biopsy could be analyzed, but blood cells weren't able to be sucked out.

After that, everyone was talking. Barry's colleagues were all trying to explain away the dry tap. It was a fixation; everyone had a theory. They meant well, but their constant questions and suggestions were overwhelming. People who weren't involved in his care would poke their heads into the room. Residents, interns, and others came in to ask, "What's his blood count?" just after we'd discussed it with his doctor. They'd rush in with news like, "He just had the CAT scan," when Barry had been wheeled in from the procedure twenty minutes before.

They treated him as if they were on rounds, listing diagnostic characteristics: "A thirty-year-old guy with a white count of six thousand, a mediastinal mass, and a dry tap." The thing was, this was my brother. I was sleep-deprived and lost, constantly thinking, *I know; I know. Why are you telling me this again?*

For the family, everything a doctor says about their loved one is personal. These weren't even my brother's doctors. I listened to their bantering, bickering analyses and felt so dismayed. I wished they could leave it at the door. I'm sure that most if not all of them were just trying to be helpful. Many of the residents and attending doctors were more experienced with leukemia than I was, but their whirling opinions and comments were dizzying.

There were too many cooks in the kitchen. For Barry, the patient, I'm sure it was even worse. Barry was a good doctor and loved discussing cases, but he never participated in these debates. There he was, in serious condition, waiting to find out what was coming next. What kind of leukemia did he have? What would treatment look like? Was he going to die? Did he need a bone marrow transplant right away, or would chemotherapy be the best first step? Such a crazy question was now a reality. At his bedside, his colleagues were going through their depersonalized, knee-jerk reactions. They were right in front of him; he couldn't escape. All the while, his four-week-old son was at home. Barry wasn't sure he would ever see his baby boy again.

I had to learn to be a border guard at the threshold of my brother's room. During his short time waiting at home before coming in to be admitted, Barry had only chosen to tell a few people outside of his immediate family that he was sick, but now all of his colleagues knew. At the very least, we had to keep out the people who weren't absolutely necessary. It became our job, as Barry's family, to protect his privacy when he didn't have the strength to do so himself. I couldn't care for Barry as his doctor, but I had to do so as his brother. Whether that meant keeping his room more private or watching TV with him late at night, I had to help somehow.

My brother needed the best possible care. I needed to make sure he was getting it. When Barry saw the initial blood work that indicated leukemia, he called Dr. K., an attending hematologist/oncologist at Montefiore. Dr. K. was a local guy. He was good-looking and well dressed. He walked through the hospital like it was the street on which he'd grown up, smiling and greeting people. He greeted everyone—all the nurses, cafeteria staff, and maintenance workers—by name. To me, it was astounding how much respect Dr. K. had earned from everyone at all levels of the hospital. People considered him a celebrity, or so it appeared to me. Even though he was a highly regarded specialist in the competitive world of academic medicine, he never acted like he was more important than any other person around him. He was just so nice. That matters a lot in the hospital. When you're in there dealing with difficult situations, the way you handle yourself can make a big difference to the people around you.

When Barry initially talked to Dr. K. about treating him, he asked him, "Please tell me if I'd be better off in a designated cancer center." Barry wanted to be in a familiar place, but he knew that sometimes the best care was elsewhere. Barry was always a homebody, comfortable around familiar faces. When times got tough, he tended to stick to what he knew.

Dr. K. agreed to tell Barry if he felt like he or the institution was out of its depth. When Barry asked him, "Is this the best place for me to be?" Dr. K. responded, "Right now, yes." I think, at the time, he was right. Dr. K. assured Barry that if there came a point when the disease was outside his expertise, he would tell Barry. We were all relieved that Dr. K. was willing to let Barry in on his thoughts and his confidence.

That first day, we had to wait for diagnostic clarity and a plan of action. We didn't yet know what kind of leukemia he had. It was one of two major subclasses of acute-onset leukemias, but it would take more time for the result of one particular test to come back. In my mind, I started playing the odds, guessing at the lesser of the evils. Was it AML, acute myelogenous leukemia, or was it ALL, acute lymphocytic leukemia? My thoughts raced with the impossible question, "Which one would *I* want?" It was crazy to be hoping for one cancer over another.

Watching the inner workings of the hospital from the perspective of a patient, the other side of the bed from my training, taught me crucial lessons about communication. I became aware that I had to do better—doctor interactions could make or break my brother's state of mind at a given moment. Barry was at his most vulnerable.

The Other Side of the Bed

I realized that patients need accuracy, understanding, and hope. Our human instinct is to comfort each other and avoid saying the hard things, but avoidance creates confusion. Patients and their families need to know precisely what is going on so they and their doctors can determine the proper treatment.

Recently, an elderly man was referred to me. He was already suffering from memory deficits when he began to have trouble swallowing. His primary-care physician referred him to me to address the new symptom. I knew I would be doing much more than that.

I met him and his wife for the first time just before the procedure. His wife arrived with a terrified look on her face.

After a few introductory questions, I asked her, "What is it that you're worried about?"

She was quiet, but I could tell she needed to talk.

I opened the conversation by saying, "Based on your husband's age alone, I'm worried about cancer. It *could* be reflux or an infection, but I'm worried about cancer." That broke the ice.

She said, "I'm worried about cancer too. But I'm worried that if you tell him he has cancer, it'll kill him."

Now that she had told me exactly what she was afraid of, I was able to adapt to her and her husband's needs.

That moment brought me back to an old adage I learned in med school: "Forget the tests; forget the chart. Just listen to and treat the patient." While it is anecdotal, it is said that's how more than 70 percent of diagnoses are made; some people might argue the number is even higher. It's all about starting the conversation that will lead to the right answers for that specific patient.

Daniel S. Mishkin, M.D.

After performing the procedure, I was pretty sure that the patient had esophageal cancer. I decided to call the couple's primary-care doctor. I told the primary-care doctor that I was still waiting for the pathology, but what I saw looked like cancer. He might be someone the wife would turn to for advice, and I wanted the couple's support system to be in place when I eventually delivered the grim news.

I told her, "The thing we were afraid of is a strong possibility." I knew fear of cancer and all its implications was at the forefront of her mind. "I don't have a CAT scan and we're still waiting on the pathology, but from what I see, this could be bad. I'll be here with you through the whole process."

"OK, what do we do now?" she asked.

I tried my best to be clear about what I did and didn't know. She and I sat together, talking for at least twenty minutes. With a physician's visit typically lasting fifteen minutes, five extra minutes can seem like an eternity. Personally, I don't mind spending the time. The problem is that a delay with one patient will cause a domino effect on my schedule. Subsequent patients will be taken in late. They'll tell me how upset they are with me for not being on schedule. Sometimes, later, they'll write this as a complaint on the physician surveys that are sent out. Yet, that time was not frivolously wasted; it was spent caring for a patient, physically and emotionally. If I'm late, it's not because I'm sitting around or off playing golf; it's because I'm trying to provide the best care I can. As a patient, you always want to be the quick and easy office visit.

Sometimes the practice of medicine just comes down to talking and listening. In medical school, when I was learning to deliver bad news, presenting options to patients was a crucial part of the curriculum. I was taught to do this as a fundamental part of patient care. For me, it really makes sense as a way to assuage concerns and empower patients. I tell patients what I'm thinking as I describe different procedures and protocols. I translate my knowledge to my patients in a way that involves them in their own care. Some patients say, "Just tell me what to do." I tell them, "Here's the option that offers the best chance for you." Even if that's all they want to hear, I still describe other treatment options in concrete, objective terms. I explain what I have and haven't recommended and why, so they can understand my reasoning. In this day and age, patients are turning to outside resources like friends, the Internet, and other less reliable sources. They need a crash course in their own diagnosis so they don't get fooled or led down a wrong path. I hope that it helps them feel some control and clarity as they begin the difficult transition from diagnosis to treatment, or from one treatment stage to the next.

When I give bad news to a patient, I often give out my cell phone number. Patients just need a chance to talk sometimes. For me, it's just part of helping them through a difficult situation. Most physicians don't do this because they're afraid that patients will abuse the privilege. It's a risk, but it's not one that I've seen backfire too many times. It has the potential to cut into a physician's precious personal time. Even physicians need time away from the job to keep up our mental health. No one can give 120 percent every day of every year; it would be a recipe for disaster.

When Barry was sick, I wanted all the information I could get. Because I was an intern in the first year of my residency and my father was a doctor, we had huge networks of resources to draw from in assessing the plan for his care. I knew how to find who the experts were and the most up-to-date treatments. I knew how to research the journals and read the textbooks to put it all together. Few patients have that much access to knowledge in the beginning. Some even get sucked into hearing other laypeople provide

Daniel Mishkin

advice that may not be relevant at all. After a long battle with a disease, though, many times patients and their families can seem like they know more than the doctor.

With devastating diagnoses, patients sometimes feel the need to seek out a second opinion. For a lot of physicians, this request sounds threatening. Doctors see it as a question of competency or trust. That defensive response is understandable, but I believe in encouraging patients who are already considering it to get that second opinion. It helps to ease their worries and build trust in the doctor-patient relationship. When patients do want a second opinion, I try to send my patients to a variety of colleagues so I'm not always referring them to one person; I want the medicine to be scientific.

Sometimes doctors need to get second opinions too. When I'm presented with a challenging case, I might call one expert on inflammatory bowel disease, or another on bile ducts or pancreas problems. On occasion I might call a "curbside consult," where I present a case to another expert and get his or her informal thoughts on it, just to give me a different perspective. Many times, other physicians call me. Whatever happens, I learn from my colleagues and build relationships with experts who together can help me to provide better patient state-of-the-art care.

3
MY BROTHER'S KEEPER

Jumping through Hoops in the Oncology Ward

As a resident, I always had the supervision of other doctors. With my brother in the bed, I felt alone. I didn't know whether I understood enough, or if the physician was telling us everything we needed to know. Just after Barry found out he had cancer, the waiting was agonizing. We were waiting for tests, and the results couldn't come quickly enough. I was hanging on to every word the attendings said, like a layperson with little medical knowledge. Only a day or so earlier, I had thought I knew so much. I was the one in the conference, answering every rapid-fire question from Dr. G. There's such a wide expanse between knowing a bit about a disease and actually having the experience of treating it. It's the difference between knowledge and expertise.

Once, in my third year of residency, I was working on a Sunday afternoon when I was paged to the cardiac pre-op floor for a code. I was supposed to be the senior person on hand when there was a code, when a

Daniel S. Mishkin, M.D.

patient was in trouble. I was the third person to arrive, and when I stepped into the room, I felt like I'd walked onto a comedy set. The patient's arms were flailing, trying to push away the nurse who was straddling his chest. At the head of the bed, the orderly was yelling, "We need help! We need help!"

The nurse was trying to do chest compressions. The orderly was trying to force an oxygen bag onto the patient's face. All the while, the patient was resisting their best efforts. It looked like the people who were supposed to be helping the patient were trying to beat him up and strangle him.

"Guys, get off him!" I screamed. I couldn't believe what I was seeing.

"No, I know what I'm doing, I just took a CPR course," said the nurse.

The patient was trying to tell them to stop, but the orderly was covering his face.

I heard the orderly say, "Sir, you don't understand. You have to let us do this or you're going to die."

They weren't saving his life; they were nearly killing him. CPR should only be done on a patient who's clinically dead: no pulse, no breath, and certainly no physical resistance. I kept yelling at them, "You have to stop! You have to stop!"—trying to get them to snap out of this trancelike state they'd entered. Soon, more people arrived in response to the code. Fortunately, the nurse stopped. I glimpsed an aha moment in her eyes. She walked to the back of the room and watched as we started to manage the case and stabilize the situation.

When the rest of us went to examine the patient, we found his ribs cracked. He had been scheduled for cardiac surgery the next day. Now that had to be postponed.

Here's what had happened: The patient had been given a medication that had caused his blood pressure to drop more than his body could easily handle. He had been in a chair, then stood with an orderly to move to the bed, when his eyes suddenly rolled back. He'd gone unconscious—briefly—so he was moved quickly to the bed. He must have come to shortly thereafter, though, because he told me later that he remembered awaking to the nurse on top of him. The nurse was so caught up in the idea that she was about to use the training she'd just received that she didn't pay attention to what was right in front of her.

There's a saying in medicine: "Before you touch an unstable patient, check your own pulse. Make sure you're thinking clearly before you do anything to someone else." The nurse had just gone through CPR training, so it was at the forefront of her mind. When the patient lost consciousness, she jumped on the bed and started doing chest compressions—even after the patient tried to convince her that he'd regained consciousness. She had failed to check her own pulse—as well as his.

My dad was a doctor, so I grew up playing in his lab and walking the patients'-floor hallways of his hospital without any reservation. As a kid I was familiar with the inside of office walls, but not the inside of patient rooms. People died there.

Still, I always knew I wanted to be a doctor. I was lucky enough to have my father around as a mentor. When I was eighteen, he advised me to volunteer at his hospital's palliative care unit, where terminally ill patients who have elected to stop treatment are cared for. As a physician, he knew that the interpersonal intricacies of medicine are impossible to learn from books. You have to gain experience to know how to act with someone who is dying.

It wasn't easy for me. I went in once a week or so, and every time, the people who had been there on my previous visit were gone. Seeing a constant turnover of patients took a toll on me.

Daniel S. Mishkin, M.D.

I had been volunteering there for a year or so when my maternal grandmother got sick. I was very close with her. She was admitted for something minor on a regular hospital floor, but I didn't want to go visit her. I was afraid I'd see her looking gravely ill like the terminal patients with whom I had worked. I didn't want to see her in that environment. Death was hiding behind those walls like a dragon in a dungeon I dared not enter.

When I did go to see her, I felt so awkward. I couldn't look past the little aspects of her hospital room, the things I'd been taught to pay attention to as a volunteer. I commented on the way her sheets were folded. I asked her if she had ice available, and if I could get her something to eat or drink. It was a defense mechanism.

Later, I confided in my brother Barry. I told him how afraid I was of seeing our grandmother ill. He reminded me that in the palliative care unit, I was seeing a skewed population. He redirected my focus and alleviated my concerns and worries.

He also told me that in order to experience the highs of taking patients back from the brink, I also had to take the lows. In those situations, though, I needed to learn to express my fears and deal with them. I couldn't just keep my emotions bottled up. With Barry's encouragement, I kept volunteering and started to address my reactions to the stressful environment. Barry always had more faith in me than I had in myself.

My grandmother got better. She came home and ended up living another twenty years. She passed away a few years ago at the ripe old age of ninety-eight (we think; we're never sure she told us her true age). Even at the age of ninety-eight, she would get down on the floor to play with my daughters, as if she were still in her fifties or sixties. She would have done anything for the family. They don't make them like they used to. She was a wonderful woman, tough as nails, and she's always been an inspiration to my family and me.

The Other Side of the Bed

A few years after my grandmother's illness, when I was a fourth-year medical student, I got a call at the hospital.

"Your grandfather's upstairs," the person said.

My grandfather? My mother's father had passed away. I didn't have much connection with my father's father.

"Who?" I asked.

"Your grandfather," the caller said, adding his name.

It was my father's father; I'd never spent much time with him.

Except for infrequent letters, my grandfather had cut my father and our family out of his life. Yet here he was. My grandfather. Upstairs in the hospital, asking for me.

I decided to go see him, but not to tell my father first. I had no idea how it would go.

I was prepared for the worst when I knocked on his door, walked in the room, and essentially introduced myself. He called me over and thanked me for coming. Then he did the strangest thing: he asked for my medical advice. I was taken aback. Here I was, a fourth-year med student, still learning to tell who was sick; I was completely out of my depth.

"What should I do?" my grandfather asked.

I didn't know why he was asking me. I didn't feel qualified to answer. I didn't even know him. I tried to say something neutral, but I was so uncomfortable. I had select knowledge, but *some* knowledge can be worse than no knowledge. As a medical student, you are not expected to take responsibility for a patient. During rounds, you'll be asked to provide information as if you were the most senior person. In reality, you have minimal knowledge and little ownership. I didn't have the expertise to know how to actually treat his disease. I could not have been his advocate. Heck, I didn't even know his medical history.

47

Daniel S. Mishkin, M.D.

I told my dad that I had seen my grandfather. Despite all that had transpired between them, my dad still loved him and came to visit him in the hospital. He was discharged soon after. I know it was a turning point in their relationship. My dad could see what was about to happen, and he desperately wanted to reconcile the relationship before things went downhill.

A few weeks later, my grandfather was readmitted—this time, to the ICU. It was clear his condition was serious. I called my dad right away, and he came straight in. He knew it could be close to the end.

Once my dad arrived, we spoke with my grandfather's attending physician. The attending was a doctor I know and trust, but someone whose demeanor doesn't convey much affect. He speaks simply and directly, without emotion. While I always appreciate clarity, his bald tone was hard to take.

He told us, "He's going to die. Probably today or tomorrow."

I'd read the chart. It was pretty clear he was in trouble. Was there really *nothing* proactive to consider? I was accustomed to the assertive Socratic teaching methods so common in medical school. I knew the senior attending was firm in his opinion, but I'd read the chart. From my book smarts, I believed that there was more he could do, that *we* could do.

I cut in, "Well, what if," and listed some options I'd come up with.

"Why are you pushing this?" the doctor asked.

"You could do more," I said. I knew my grandfather's illness was serious, but the doctor was completely dismissing viable options. Why was he so willing to write off the patient?

All of a sudden, I had jumped into making a medical decision for a family member. I'd never even spent any significant time with my grandfather before the recent turn of events, but he was still my blood relative. I didn't have a lifelong emotional tie to him, but I was sure the doctor was wrong. I felt the need to speak up.

The doctor held his ground, respectfully. He could have easily pulled rank and said something gruff and belittling; it certainly happens in teaching situations. I was far too inexperienced to go up against him, but he was fair. He was also right. My grandfather was going to die, and I had to let go. I had tunnel vision, seeing only the diagnosis and its possible treatments. The attending had a broader view. He could see the whole patient.

That was the first time I had ever been privy to a conversation about a loved one's medical care. I was wrong when I questioned the attending's judgment, but it was an automatic response, a reflex for me. It was also a rite of passage. In that moment, I felt a hint of what it would later feel like to advocate for a family member, taking responsibility for a person, not just a patient.

Most of all, that episode was a moment of growth for me. My experience with my grandfather gave me the first hint of what it felt like to sit on the patient's side of the bed. I've always had a cool head in a crisis, so I was blindsided by how emotional I felt.

If I, the physician, take a little extra time with families and patients to help them feel as knowledgeable and comfortable as possible, it's easier for all of us to work together. In long-term patient care, we need all hands on deck.

When Barry got sick, I felt crippled by my fear of the unknown. I was a resident, more knowledgeable than I'd been when my grandfather got sick, but still in training. My knowledge level fell somewhere between that of a nonmedical family member and that of the real doctors. However, some of the doctors saw me as a kid, a nuisance.

As I see it now, there's an order to medical knowledge. As a medical student, you learn who is sick, and who is not. As an intern, you learn how

Daniel S. Mishkin, M.D.

to stabilize a patient. As a resident, you learn how to treat a patient. As an attending, you learn how to take care of the entire patient for the long term. When Barry got sick, I was still an intern. I was nowhere near prepared to actively participate in the care of critical patients like my brother.

At the same time, I was learning to live in the hospital. For as much time as I had spent within those walls, on the other side of the doctor-patient divide as a student and trainee, I had no idea how chaotic a patient's room can be. In Barry's room, there was constant movement in and out: medical assistants taking his vitals, orderlies transporting him for X-rays and CAT scans, nurses checking on his IV access. On nights that I slept there with him, if I didn't get up, brush my teeth, wash my face, and change my clothes first thing, I wouldn't have a chance to do so until the day had slipped away entirely. I had to be up and ready for anything at any time. More importantly, I always had to be on my best behavior. The fact is, nurses run the hospital. It's an important lesson for physicians and patients alike to learn. I knew that I had to stay in their good graces. I had to stay calm and collected as everything spun out of control.

On Thursday, the day after Barry was admitted, he felt a little bit better. At the time of his admission, his blood had been running on empty. The multiple transfusions he had received throughout the night refilled his depleted store of blood cells and oxygen, giving him a little more energy. He decided he wanted to let a few friends in to visit who were in the hospital, working overnight call. I felt relieved. It's hard to be in the hospital at night. Barry felt terrified of being alone there, and I wanted to comfort him. He was a social person; the fact that he wanted to see people was a reminder of normal Barry, healthy Barry. It was a small moment of catharsis, even laughter, in the midst of a harrowing eternity of twenty-four hours. The room became a bit crowded, and perhaps a little loud, and one of the nurses

The Other Side of the Bed

got upset with us. It was nighttime, and the nurse was inadvertently bothered. I'm not sure what additional work it might've created for him, but he was indignant at the deviation from the norm.

I thought little of it at the time, but the next morning, the same nurse retaliated against my brother. Barry was having the usual reaction that we would all have, wanting some semblance of normalcy, if possible. After having been displaced to the hospital, undergoing multiple procedures and tests, Barry wanted to take a shower. Without any medical reason, when Barry was ready, the nurse told him, "You can't." He gave no justification, and he stood firm when Barry challenged him. It was nurse against patient. Barry was no longer the doctor in charge of overseeing the treatment; he was now the patient.

The fact is, the previous day, Barry had arranged for his own admission to the hospital. *He* had ordered the blood work; *he* had read the tests. He'd run the results by an attending he trusted and when it came time for his admission, he was calling the shots. The medical resident who took his history started shaking, he was so nervous. Even with his blood levels at such a low state and his oxygen dropping, Barry was an educator. My brother calmed the resident down and reviewed the differential with him during the admission. Now Barry was holding on to his autonomy as much as he could. But he was on the wrong side of the bed.

The nurse wouldn't let him have the basic dignity of hygiene, and Barry was demoralized. He looked at me and started to cry. It was the first time I saw Barry cry since he'd been admitted. I think he must have cried in his apartment when he first heard that he had cancer (I know I would have), but once in the hospital, he was so busy with doctors, visitors, and tests that he had not broken down.

After the incident with the nurse, Barry realized that he didn't have the capacity to advocate for himself; he was far too sick to retain his autonomy.

Daniel S. Mishkin, M.D.

I couldn't get the nurse to let Barry shower, but I knew that I had to do more to protect my brother. There were certain things he *was* able to hold on to: He kept wearing scrubs, rather than a hospital gown. He tried to keep the well-earned measures of dignity and respect as a physician that he could—things neither of us had ever thought about before. We'd taken care of plenty of patients, but neither of us knew if there were even criteria to allow a patient to shower. It had never been on the list of details we would pay attention to. This was the beginning of our new curriculum in medicine. At night, we watched TV and talked, just to keep his mind off of things.

That night, Friday night, the doctor came in with the diagnosis: acute T-cell lymphocytic leukemia (ALL). He proposed a treatment plan; chemo would start the next day. This is an incredibly aggressive cancer in adults. We had to act fast.

The reality was, I didn't have time to research the specific treatment. The doctor told me so very plainly that we had to hit him hard with this first induction regimen, right away.

ALL, the kind of leukemia Barry had, is vicious and virulent. Cancer, in general, is an abnormal, unceasing growth of cells. Normal cells have feedbacks that keep them from continuing to grow. Cancer cells don't act like normal cells that respond to normal feedback mechanisms. They replicate continuously, uninhibited by any automatic shutoff mechanisms. All cancers are dangerous because of their ability to interrupt normal bodily functions, but each kind has its own pathways that regulate its growth. Each variety of cancer can even have multiple growth pathways and timelines.

Each kind of cancer has different characteristics. With breast cancer, for instance, abnormal cells grow in the breast tissue, forming tumors that destroy everything in their path. The tumors attack organs, nerves, and blood vessels. Leukemia is cancer of the blood. It infiltrates a patient's bone marrow, where the components of blood are produced: white blood cells, platelets, and red blood cells. Leukemia depletes the bone marrow so the body can't fight off infections, can't clot, and, because of diminished hemoglobin, can't even carry oxygen. We had to move rapidly.

Different chemotherapy regimens target different kinds of replication pathways, the ways in which cells reproduce. Some regimens are better for colon cancer, some are better for prostate cancer, and some are better for leukemia. With any protocol there can be drastic side effects. Doctors have to balance the cancer's virulence against the chemo's destruction.

As an intern I didn't know anything about cancer treatment protocols, but I had a resource at my disposal who did. Before I'd left Montreal, Dr. G., the attending hematologist I'd worked with, had told me to keep in touch about my brother's condition. I was eager to seek her counsel. I dialed her number and told her the plan.

She told me, "Honestly, most of these protocols for this disease are pretty much the same. Six of one, half a dozen of the other. It's not necessarily the one I would choose, but it's probably OK. Just start the treatment."

I thanked her for her guidance and hung up feeling uneasy. Maybe this wasn't the right protocol, but at that point, it didn't seem like we had a choice. We had a decision and a treatment plan from a physician my brother knew and trusted. I didn't want to suggest getting a second opinion and waiting to start treatment because I knew how serious Barry's condition was. I thought it would be OK. I had no reason to think otherwise.

On Friday afternoon, two days after the initial diagnosis, my father and sister arrived from Montreal. My father had stayed behind initially to arrange his medical practice in such a way that his patients' care would not

Daniel S. Mishkin, M.D.

be disrupted. As a doctor, he knew intellectually that Barry was sick, but his physical distance and need to stay focused on his own practice made it more difficult for him to comprehend how really ill Barry was, until he arrived at his bedside. On his way to New York, he stopped at a duty-free liquor store. My dad's not a huge drinker, but he appreciates a good Scotch, and he and Barry loved tasting it together. When he arrived at the hospital, he pulled the bottle out of his bag to show Barry his new find in the hopes of drinking it with him later. Barry looked at him, astonished.

"I'm getting chemo," he said. "I can't drink."

Right there, amber-gleaming bottle in his hand, my father broke down in tears. A new reality had begun.

Barry started chemo the next day. Meanwhile, I was working out how to get time off from my residency work, playing bouncer in the doorway, and trying to get a handle on treatment protocols. This was no vacation. My father had the medical knowledge, but he was way too emotional. He told me he couldn't get involved in analyzing Barry's treatment. My mother, who has strong medical instincts, agreed. My parents felt too close to it, and they thought we should trust the specialists.

I was a medical resident, but on the subject of chemotherapy, I knew little more than a layperson. When most people hear "chemo," they think of a vague thing that's going to ravage the body with side effects and hopefully destroy the cancer, but they don't have any idea what the treatment is. Is it an IV drip, a pill? At what dose? For how long? How frequently?

I clung to what I did know: how to do medical research and digest it, then ask others to lend their expertise. I had access to the journals, so I began reading studies and figuring out who was running the active trials on acute lymphocytic leukemia (ALL). Through my reading, I began to become acquainted with the specifics of the disease, its treatments, and the names of physicians at different institutions. I was fortunate to have had the knowledge base to do this kind of research into treatment protocols when my brother got sick. It takes specialized knowledge and training. For nonmedical family members, the whole process can be maddening. Doctor talk and medical jargon are a distinct discourse, and to talk with the heavy hitters, you need to be fluent. The average layperson could try to fake it, but it would never fly.

Why had Barry's doctor chosen that particular protocol, and why did the hematologist I consulted say she might have advised another choice? It was a subtle question, not an objection, but I had to know more.

I did some reading to get comfortable with the general characteristics of ALL, then started cold-calling the clinician researchers. I called people at MD Anderson in Houston, Fred Hutchinson in Seattle, and Sloan Kettering in New York. I didn't know any of them, but I knew what to say when they picked up the phone.

I started each conversation by telling them my background and my brother's situation: "I'm an intern, I'm reading your ALL studies, and my brother is sick," I told them. "I am a physician as well. My father is also a doctor, and my brother is currently a chief resident."

I was a young trainee, but I had some professional clout thanks to my family. I was also in a terrible situation, and they really sympathized. That was enough to get me past the assistants and administrators answering the phones. At that point, these gatekeepers would either have the physician call me back or give me permission to call when he or she would be free to talk.

When that time finally came, I'd ask, "Can I tell you what's going on? May I ask your advice?"

Right off the bat, they'd know that a member of the medical club, the inner circle, was calling to ask for help. I was up front with my information,

Daniel S. Mishkin, M.D.

and I communicated as directly as I could. I was a family member, but I was also a doctor. In this community, we speak a common language and struggle with shared life-and-death issues every day. We've jumped through the same hoops to get into medicine; it creates a real bond between strangers. Everyone I called was generous with his or her time. It's almost like calling a fraternity member whom you can contact even if you've never met. Most doctors are really out to help patients and do the right thing by them. Unfortunately, it is usually our fear of lawsuits that limits how much we discuss in such situations.

I spent as much time as possible speaking with physician experts and consulting Dr. G. in Montreal, as well as other clinician researchers elsewhere. Each one helped me piece together the facts. I'd find a new insight from one expert, then ask another for her thoughts. The amalgamation of opinions was starting to add up. Soon, my unease was confirmed: Barry was receiving treatment that may not have been the best for his specific diagnosis.

The protocol that Barry's physician had decided on was correct for the majority of ALL patients and was being investigated. However, my research revealed that a paradigm shift was under way, and that it was increasingly thought that the treatment course suggested by Barry's doctor might not be the most effective. For T-cell acute lymphocytic leukemias, patients need stronger chemo. The chemo regimen Barry had been given included weak dosing—far too weak to do what would produce the best long-term results. Leukemia is aggressive. Imagine if you had a huge cockroach in your kitchen and you tried spraying it with ant killer. It wouldn't do anything. This same scenario was potentially playing out in my brother's body, and we had no clue.

Barry had chosen his attending physician. He knew the man, and he liked him. At first, that was all I needed to know; I could trust Barry with anything. But when I really looked at my brother, I knew he wasn't himself.

His eyes were sunken and his cheeks were hollow. His skin was pallid and gray. He couldn't keep up with what was going on around him. Though I trusted the doctor's initial assessments, given the urgency of Barry's chemo treatment, I found myself struggling with increasing doubts over the next few weeks. What was done was done, but we needed to figure out what we were going to do for the next courses of chemo. I needed to figure out what we could do better without alarming my brother. I didn't want to make waves if I didn't have to.

4
HIERARCHY IN MEDICINE

At the end of his first round of chemo, Barry's bone marrow was extremely depleted. A round of chemo starts with extremely aggressive doses of medication, which wipe out the patient's bone marrow. Then, over the course of the treatment, the medication is tapered off and the bone marrow is given the chance to recover. With any kind of chemo, patients experience bone marrow depletion. With leukemia, it's not only an aspect of the disease; it's also a side effect of the treatment. At the end of that first round, the levels of all of Barry's blood cell types were low.

He needed to hold off on transfusions for as long as he could. The doctors wanted to let his bone marrow regrow and replenish his blood before the next round of chemo. With every transfusion, there's the risk of infection, as well as the incremental immune intolerance that we build up to others' blood. With every transfusion, the body develops antibodies that fight off the next one. We didn't want that to happen; we still had a long road ahead. As all of Barry's doctors had told me, this was a marathon, not a sprint.

Daniel S. Mishkin, M.D.

In a course of chemotherapy, it's common for a patient's blood levels to drop steeply at first, then build back up as their bone marrow reconstitutes. By this point, his levels had dropped and remained low for a while. Every day we were asking, "What are the counts today? Have they increased from yesterday?"

For a series of agonizing days, his platelets hovered around ten thousand; this number is a benchmark. If a patient has at least ten thousand platelets, he can wait to get more platelet transfusions, as long as he is not bleeding. Below ten thousand, the risk of having a cerebral hemorrhage is significant. Bleeding in the brain can be lethal. A patient shouldn't be very active, to avoid any consumption of the limited platelets in the body. We all watched over him and did what we could to avoid any unintentional trauma that could use up those precious platelets.

One evening, a medical assistant came in to take his blood pressure. She affixed the cuff around his arm, then proceeded to pump the cuff up to 200 mmHg, far higher and far tighter than was necessary. Then I saw that she didn't even have her stethoscope on. As she reached down into her cart to get it, I hurdled over the bed to release the cuff.

"What are you doing?!" she cried.

She had no idea what *she* was doing. His blood pressure was around 110. There was no need to pump the cuff so high. With the too-tight blood pressure cuff, she was pinching him hard, causing his body to expend precious platelets. At first, I tried to explain to her that this was inappropriate, but she shooed me away, saying she had it under control.

"I know what I'm doing," she claimed. That was it. I'd had enough.

"Don't touch my brother!" I demanded. "Get away from him."

If looks could kill, she might've killed me. As she tried to protest, a nurse heard us from the hallway. I explained what had happened and refused to move from his side until the issue was resolved. In this case, I was lucky that a simple solution was reached: I could take his vitals—blood pressure, pulse, and temperature. When I was there, it was OK, but I couldn't always be there; no one ever can. Other people would also have to take his vitals, but they had to have more experience than the medical assistant I'd encountered. I also felt the need to protect other patients. I can only hope she took this criticism as constructive and not just the concern of an overprotective family member.

A chain is only as strong as its weakest link. In the hospital, there are so many links in the chain; everyone has to work up to a high standard when patients' lives hang in the balance. Having a medical assistant with minimal knowledge in this case meant that, as smart or polite as she was on any other issue, she didn't know the repercussions of her actions. She didn't even realize that she didn't know what she was doing.

Medical mistakes happen, often beyond our control. Doctors always have to remain on the offensive against error. It takes a lifetime to build a reputation, but it only takes a second to destroy one.

In between Barry's subsequent rounds of chemo, I went back to Montreal to work consecutive shifts. I was working through my personal baggage and exhaustion. I was on duty on the hematology-oncology floor, and there was a twenty-four-year-old man with leukemia similar to my brother's. His platelets were at twenty-four thousand. He had just been diagnosed—the day after being admitted—and was still waiting on treatment decisions. When would he start treatment? We didn't yet know, but it would most likely be the next day.

His platelets were very low, but he still had to start chemo. His numbers would only get worse. He needed platelets. I told the senior resident so.

"What are you talking about? You need to calm down," said the resident.

I felt like I was being dismissed and fought back.

"He's only going to get worse."

It was true. There was no chance that the dip would flatten out or improve at this point. Why risk it? Transfuse him now. We had to think of the patient's next weeks and months.

"You're personalizing it, you can't do this on every case," the senior resident told me. He wouldn't authorize a transfusion. He was right in the textbook sense, but I felt that I was correct based on my own personal knowledge of the disease and its behavior. I was so angry. I'd been to hell and back with Barry. I'd seen this problem close-up, and even though the other resident was more senior than I, I knew that I was right in my heart. Based on the protocols, however, he was right. I definitely would have agreed with him, if not for my own heavy baggage.

"You don't know anything," I said.

We had no way to know what was to transpire later that evening. About three hours later, in the middle of the night, the patient slipped on the way to the bathroom. He hit his head, bled out into his brain, and died—all while I was on call. Would the platelets have prevented his death? I can't say. Maybe. Did his presenting numbers call for it? Without a doubt, no. It was terrible luck in a bad situation. While looking at the whole patient and where he was in the treatment plan, I had thought he'd needed the boost. Now, here we were in the early hours of the morning telling his family that he'd died even before starting treatment. It was a disaster.

"I don't understand," I remember his mother saying. "His numbers were OK last night. He was supposed to be starting treatment. How could this happen?"

As I've mentioned, Barry initially felt some trepidation about receiving treatment at Montefiore, the hospital where he worked. There were pros and cons. He knew everyone there. He'd known them for years. They knew him too, through medical school and then into his internship and residency. When Barry got sick, he was chief resident. Would his colleagues be the ones to give him a fighting chance at survival? Would his personal connection to them help or hinder his care? Would there be some comfort in receiving treatment by and among the people he knew, or would it feel like his private struggle was on display for all to see?

I wasn't looking for the hospital to make mistakes. These were Barry's colleagues, who had much more experience than I did. More than that, the people there had done a great deal to help my family. For instance, a couple of days into his hospitalization, they admitted Barry into a private, double-bedded room, but they didn't fill the second bed. That meant that whoever was there overnight with Barry had a bed to sleep in. Not a sofa, not a foldout couch, not a futon; they kept open a bed for us—and many nights, it was for me. He never wanted to be alone at night, and I couldn't let him feel that fear.

The private room also meant that we didn't have to deal with one of the most awkward aspects of the hospital stay. Hospital curtains are obviously not soundproof. But people, and especially people in stressful situations, forget that. I've heard people talking about me behind curtains, and I've seen patients make remarks that they think another person can't hear. It's hard to get used to not having privacy. Luckily, at least at first, Barry was spared that experience.

The hospital's generosity didn't stop there; they gave us an apartment in residency housing across the street during a holiday week when the entire family was there at the same time. Someone even arranged for us to have an extra parking pass—a scarce commodity that normally cost more than a hundred dollars per month. Our family gained comfort and ease because

Daniel S. Mishkin, M.D.

Barry knew the people there, and they went out of their way to care for him. People also looked at Barry, an otherwise healthy young man prior to his diagnosis, and grasped that any one of them could have been in his position; they wanted to treat him and his family as they would have wanted to have been treated.

Once, early in Barry's first round of chemo, I remember waking up and seeing Dr. K. standing in the room. He was at Barry's bedside, talking to him about issues other than his medical condition.

"What's wrong?" I asked and sprang out of bed.

Barry just laughed. Dr. K. had been called in to care for another patient on Barry's floor. He'd stopped by Barry's room for a social visit, just to check in, at 12:30 a.m. It was a caring thing to do and we were all comforted by this gesture of kindness.

The more I researched, though, the more certain I became that the treatment protocol Barry was on was outdated; he wasn't getting the best chance at survival. I was sure that Barry was on a suboptimal treatment protocol—sure enough that I was ready to tell him. I had spoken with other physicians who were considered leaders in the field, physicians at other centers who specialized in exactly Barry's kind of cancer.

By the end of the first round of chemo, I had the research, and I began to raise my concerns. I had to; my brother's life was at stake. First, I talked to Barry. He tried to assuage my worry, but I had the research to back up my argument. He didn't have the strength to do the legwork himself. Again, he had to trust me. He didn't want to hear any questions raised about his treatment plan; he had faith in his doctors, and this was a good hospital. Nevertheless, he agreed to let me try to talk to the medical team in the hopes we could collaborate using our combined information and come up with the most effective treatment plan for him.

"Go ahead and talk to them," he told me.

I did. I told Dr. K. that I wanted to talk about the protocol and whether there might be some potential changes. I told him, "I've found some new literature." I tried to be insistent but calm. He'd seen me there, so many nights, stationed as Barry's sidekick and protector. He knew I wouldn't back down.

"OK," Dr. K. told me. He agreed to discuss the studies on medication and dosing that I'd found. He told me that he'd schedule as much time as I needed. Initially, he was very receptive.

We set the meeting for a Friday morning. Barry was home from the hospital for a few days, being treated as an outpatient between his first and second rounds of chemo. My dad flew in from Montreal that Thursday night. Even though he had stepped back from most of Barry's medical decisions, he knew he had to be present for this, as he anticipated this was going to be a difficult decision. I so appreciated his support and guidance.

In the morning I put on jeans like I always did to go to the hospital. My dad chided me.

"Daniel, put on a pair of pants. Put on a shirt and tie."

I did as he said.

I knew this meeting was our chance to save Barry. I thought my case was clear. I thought Dr. K. and the doctors would listen to me. At least, I thought, they would be willing to look at the papers I found and the notes from my conversations with world-renowned experts on this specific diagnosis and his exact issues.

A shirt and tie helped boost my confidence and showed respect, but my faith lay in my file box. It was packed full of expert studies. For weeks I'd been carrying around my box full of folders, teeming with the literature that had led me to my convictions. If the doctors would just listen, I was certain

Daniel S. Mishkin, M.D.

they would agree with my conclusion that the protocol they were using was out-of-date. They would be willing to change his regimen, and they'd see that the odds could improve significantly. I did not care who happened to be correct. All I wanted was to see Barry survive this terrible ordeal. I had worked so hard to learn about the disease and familiarize myself with the most current research. This was our best shot.

After Dr. K. examined Barry in the examination room, we all then moved to Dr. K.'s office. But once we sat down with Dr. K., Barry sized things up.

He turned to me and said, "You take over." He then grabbed his Discman and walked into the hall to wait it out. He used to do this: put on music and go "into a zone" when he was stressed. It helped him to get into a better place when he needed to check out from something emotionally taxing. I remember when he would get lumbar punctures or bone marrow biopsies, he would just put on his headphones. Essentially, he would go into a trance. Without any medication or sedation, he would journey to another place. Afterward, he would have little recollection of the procedure. He was amazing at escaping from horrific situations.

Dr. K. turned to me.

"OK, so what is it that you wanted to tell me?"

"It appears that other regimens may be better suited for the specific type of ALL that Barry has," I said.

I saw Dr. K.'s eyes tighten and his chest puff.

"I've seen some literature that shows that the protocol you're using doesn't have great results for this type of ALL," I continued, trying to show him the study I was referencing.

It was not long before Dr. K. stopped me.

"What year are you again?" he interrupted. "Aren't you an intern?"

Had he not noticed me during the past month of treatment? At first, I was confused by the question. Then, I realized that he wasn't trying to get to know me. He was asking that question for another reason.

"Yes," I responded. "I'm a first-year resident, an intern, but that's not why I'm saying the dose is too low. These experts at MD Anderson and Memorial Sloan Kettering say—" I held out a paper and tried to show him, but he cut me off.

Dr. K. continued, "Look, I've been doing this a long time. You're an intern; you're getting lost in the studies. I can see the forest for the trees."

I was ready for this. I showed him my box of papers. It was full of all the most recent literature on Barry's specific kind of ALL. I had narrowed down the wide range of research on the different manifestations of the disease to these most recent, most pertinent papers. Had Dr. K. even read them? We didn't just want a good treatment plan for ALL in general, but rather, the best treatment plan for the specific type of ALL that Barry had.

I had two copies of each paper: one copy with my copious notes and highlighting, and another clean copy for Dr. K.

I told him, "Yes, you have the experience. Barry trusts you. Just look at these studies and you'll see; we want your experience. We need your help to further clarify the information."

Dr. K. shook his head. At this point, I was incredulous. I felt like I was being dismissed outright.

He said something to the effect of, "Leave them and I'll review them, but for now, we're staying on the same regimen."

I wonder if he did review them. And if he didn't, what might have changed if he had.

Looking back, it is my suspicion that he couldn't accept that he was wrong, especially when someone so far below him in the medical hierarchy

Daniel S. Mishkin, M.D.

was saying so. The pecking order is so ingrained. He might not have thought of it this way, but as I saw it, he was out to prove that he was right from the start, no matter what—possibly at my brother's expense. As I have said, I really believed he meant the best for Barry, but my being hopeful was not enough for my brother.

At the same time, I think Dr. K. wanted to give good clinical advice. Barry was just so sick, and Dr. K. had a lot of experience in dealing with patients in this state. Barry needed him.

Even though it is my opinion that Dr. K. refused to listen to anything I said, he was still in charge of Barry's treatment. I felt strongly that Dr. K. was wrong about the chemo protocol, but what could we do? I didn't think we could transfer hospitals quickly enough for Barry to continue with his second round of chemo on schedule. I was crushed. We were stuck with Dr. K. for now. I guess I was hoping for him to reassess the situation so that we could continue to keep Barry in a familiar place. This was looking less likely. It felt like I'd been sprinting to try to save my brother, only to run straight into a brick wall. We'd entered the meeting feeling like we had a promising way forward, then left having gained no ground.

That moment of defeat has stuck with me throughout my career. It's probably why I'm so open to patients seeking second opinions. I don't personalize it; if they're having doubts about their care, then I, as a physician, have to respect those doubts. However, some patients ask for third and fourth opinions, and usually, those are not helpful.

We knew things had to change, but we didn't know how the change would come about. What would we tell Barry? We decided to wait for him to ask us. It happened later that night. When he finally asked, I told him how Dr. K. had responded to my pleas; he broke down in tears.

At this point, Barry started looking at the studies himself to see what we had been talking about. He saw what I saw: the possibility for a better outcome using an entirely different protocol from the one he was on. He couldn't believe that the doctor he had trusted implicitly was now unwilling to explore the possibility of other treatments.

He had to switch hospitals. It was a terrible prospect because we had no idea how long that might take. Could it happen before the next round of chemo? How much more time would we lose in the fight against Barry's cancer?

I knew we would go to a specialized cancer-treatment center. I had already been in contact with the senior experienced physician who was recommended to me; Dr. V. specialized in ALL. The other doctors I'd talked to had told me that he was the best leukemia specialist for Barry's case in New York.

While I was doing my pre-meeting research, Dr. V. was very helpful. He was generous with his advice, and he was willing to listen to me. We couldn't take Barry far; he was way too sick from the first round of chemo and subsequent infections. We had to stay in New York, and the option we had seemed like a good one. We felt lucky.

The Monday after our meeting with Dr. K., I called Dr. V. I thought I might be able to convince him to officially take on Barry as a patient right away. In hindsight, I know that what I was asking was impossible. In my own practice, I never take on a complex outpatient transfer until I've seen at least the most important test results and developed my own evaluation of the condition. I would never trust someone else's readings and assessments. I have to do the analysis myself, and so did Dr. V. There wouldn't be time for him to do so before Barry had to begin his next round of chemo.

When he gave me that difficult news, Dr. V. also gave me good advice, even if it was hard to hear. He said to me, "Listen, do you want to do your brother a service? Keep him at the same hospital for another month, and then transfer him after the next round. I haven't seen everything myself. I have to go through all the records. I'm not going to do it tonight. I can't do it tomorrow. He's stuck there until I do. Don't rush this."

We had to think in terms of Barry's long-term care. If he was going to beat this, it wouldn't be with overnight decisions. Dr. V. was right: we didn't have time to go through all the testing before Barry's next round of induction-phase chemo.

When I broke the news to my brother, he sighed, resigned to the tough weeks to come.

"We just have to keep a low profile," he said. He didn't want to make waves within his own workplace given the decision to transfer care.

Going into it, the next round of chemo was really not ideal. We had to spend another series of weeks with Dr. K., the doctor in whom I'd lost confidence. He had also lost confidence in us; he must have known that we were in the process of removing Barry from his care. We tried to keep things cordial and stay out of each other's way, but it was difficult to keep things calm. Barry's life was at stake.

Barry's body had taken a real beating in the first round of chemo. This second round was another induction-phase chemo, the strongest kind (even though we knew it wasn't strong enough). Again, it would deplete his bone marrow. Again, all of us would spend the next weeks worrying over small changes in his blood levels. There were always so many factors involved.

During this second round of chemo, I kept working to learn more about Barry's leukemia. One major aspect of the disease that I began to learn more about was its many prognosticators. Prognosticators are characteristics of a disease in a specific patient that are reliable predictors of patient outcomes. We refer to positively indicating predictors as "good prognosticators" and negatively indicating predictors as "bad prognosticators."

Barry's disease had a number of good prognosticators for ALL. I don't know if these still hold true today, but back then, the experts had found that certain characteristics of his cancer's presentation were good prognosticators: a mediastinal mass (a fullness seen on the chest X-ray, which he had), a patient age under thirty (he was thirty-one), a low white blood cell count (which he had), and a clean bone marrow biopsy at thirty days (for which we were waiting on results). He was in a statistically good group. When you're in there fighting for your life, these are the things you cling to. You need hope.

There was one leukemia prognosticator, though, that had a distinctly poor indication: the Philadelphia chromosome. It's a genetic mutation in the cancer cells in which parts of chromosomes 9 and 22 get transposed onto each other. Its presence in leukemia patients drops a patient's chance of survival significantly—from about 45–50 percent to 25–30 percent. If a patient's disease is Philadelphia chromosome-positive, chemo alone usually doesn't work. The treatment plan would switch to an early bone marrow transplant, rather than saving that option as a backup plan.

Early in Barry's second round of chemo, he was being treated as an outpatient. I was back in Montreal. Any time he wasn't hospitalized, I worked as much as I could to make up for the time I was away. All in all, Barry's numbers were looking good. We were cautiously encouraged by the preliminary results of the thirty-day bone marrow check, and his blood was holding strong.

On one of these days while I was away, Barry went to the clinic to receive his chemotherapy infusion. Dr. K. came in. He sat down next to Barry on the end of the bed and started talking with him, just socially to start, which Barry thought was strange given the tension between Dr. K. and our family. We were trying to get Barry through this round and out

Daniel S. Mishkin, M.D.

the door before we burned any bridges, but this raised the hair on the back of his neck.

Dr. K. started doing a thorough physical exam. Barry was confused. Why was Dr. K. doing an in-depth physical exam so long after diagnosis? Sure, things can change, but they usually show up in the test numbers. We rarely need to take the significant time to go through a full hands-on exam, and he'd undergone one not long ago.

By the time Dr. K. had finished and sat down again at the foot of Barry's bed, Barry was petrified.

Dr. K. took Barry's hand and said, "We need to talk."

Barry's mind immediately went to the hospital transfer. He told me later that he'd wondered, *What else is going on? What did Daniel do?* I was always his little brother, always the one to blame. He'd thought like this all the time, even before he was sick.

Instead, Dr. K. said, "I'm sorry, but your Philadelphia chromosome test is positive."[1] Barry had been feeling so encouraged, and it seemed like he was moving in the right direction, but this news meant that his chances for survival were slim. He knew that with a positive Philadelphia chromosome, the leukemia doesn't respond to chemo alone. He knew that if this test was positive, he would have to undergo a bone marrow transplant. Barry told me that Dr. K.'s eyes welled up with tears when he told him the news. I am confident he really cared for my brother and wanted only the best for him.

As soon as Dr. K. left the room, Barry flew into a panic. He started shouting at my mom, who was there with him.

"Call Daniel," he told her. As Mom fumbled around with the international calling card we used to call back and forth from Canada to the United States, his paranoia took over.

---

1 Barry's Philadelphia chromosome assessment was performed on the day-thirty bone marrow biopsy because the first bone marrow biopsy was a dry tap.

"Forget the card! Spend a few extra bucks!" he said.

"Calm down," Mom said.

They reached me right away.

"I'm going to die," Barry told me. It was the first time I could recall him uttering those words.

"Barry, you have to relax," I said.

I had a hunch that the test was wrong. I'd done my research: for Barry's kind of leukemia, a positive Philadelphia chromosome would've been a one-in-a-million case. I remembered my previous discussions with experts.

"It's a case report," I told him. "It's nearly impossible."

However impossible it may have seemed to me, I had to figure out what the test was actually telling us. My brother was depending on me to step in and figure out what was actually going on—never mind that I was hundreds of miles away, working on my own patients at another hospital.

Dr. K. was taking the result as a conclusion, but I took it as my job to probe further. We needed to find a mistake or we were in trouble. First, I called Dr. V. at the cancer treatment center. To this day, I can't believe he kept taking my calls.

I told him what had happened and why I thought the test was a false positive.

"Relax. There's no way," said Dr. V. Then, he rattled off all the other bad prognosticators that would go along with a Philadelphia chromosome in this kind of leukemia. Barry had none of them. He also remarked that Barry had a T-cell, not a B-cell, form that normally goes along with the Philadelphia chromosome. Dr. V. told me what to do next.

"Order FISH, and we'll prove that we're right" he said.

Fluorescent in situ hybridization: I had heard of it, but I didn't know much about it at the time. The test looks for gene changes in cells, and it

Daniel S. Mishkin, M.D.

would be able to detect the presence of a Philadelphia chromosome. As soon as I got off the phone, I ran upstairs to talk to the hematologist who had been advising me since the day Barry was diagnosed.

"If this guy, Dr. V., says it's a false positive, it's a false positive," she said. She knew his work. She encouraged me to go ahead and order the FISH.

Now, I was a doctor in a different hospital, in a different country. I didn't have jurisdiction to order this test. We called up Montefiore and asked to be connected to the lab. I got through to the person who'd conducted the test.

"I'm Dr. Mishkin, and I'm calling about my brother. I have to ask you a personal favor."

"Sure," she said.

"Here's the thing: you can hang up on me right now, but I have some questions to ask you about this test."

I still can't believe that the lab tech stayed on the line. I told her that I had doubts about the Philadelphia chromosome test, and I explained why I thought it could be a false positive. The other bad prognosticators just weren't there.

"That makes sense," she said. She went on to explain in technical terms, which I honestly did not completely understand, that it appeared positive, but there was enough doubt that in the correct clinical picture, it still might be a false positive. With this additional information, she suggested that we'd better run a secondary test to confirm.

I couldn't believe it.

"Wait a second. Can you run a secondary test—a FISH test?"

"Yes, that's exactly what I was thinking."

It was so simple. How was it so simple? Why hadn't anybody else followed up to confirm the reading before giving Barry such horrible news?

I asked her, "Did anyone else call you to talk about this test result?"

"No," she replied. "Do you want me to run the FISH?"

"Yes," I said. "Do you need an order?"

"No, I can take care of it," she said.

I hung up and immediately called my brother. He was still at the infusion center where he was receiving chemo.

I told him, "Relax, Barry; relax. It's probably OK. There's still a very, very slim chance it was positive—a case report, really—but they're running another test just to confirm. The tech told me she thought it was probably negative the first time. I'll call Dr. K."

I heard his sigh of relief, then heard him say, "Don't call Dr. K."

"I have to call him, or he'll do the wrong treatment," I said.

I had to confront him. I paged him—something only another doctor can do. The operator paged him while I waited, on hold, for him to pick up the line.

When he picked up, he said, "I figured you would find me today. This is big news." He was sincere, friendly, and compassionate.

I, however, was not.

"Yes, we do need to talk," I said. I proceeded to relay the information I had learned from speaking to Dr. V. and then to the tech in the lab. The further I progressed in the narrative, the more enraged I became.

"I'm the intern; you're the attending. You should've known this was a one-in-a-million chance. You should've checked with the lab."

I was arrogant and misguided, but he was wrong. He knew it. He was humbled.

In hindsight, the same problem could happen to any physician—but it shouldn't. We take lab reports as if they are final. If a CT scan is performed and the report comes back as normal, the physician rarely calls the radiologist to ask him or her to review it again. Today, this doubling back would be nearly impossible in our already overloaded daily schedules.

Daniel S. Mishkin, M.D.

However, in this case, there were two red flags. The first is that, with such a crucial issue, it should always be confirmed. The second is that the pieces of the patient's presentation just didn't fit. At this point, it was vital to seek out other doctors who saw my brother's rare form of leukemia regularly, not infrequently, as I suspect was the case here. My brother deserved that extra effort—just as all patients do.

Dr. K. and I had a hard time getting along after that, but I knew that I had done the right thing for my brother. Had I not followed up on the test result and asked the right questions, Barry's treatment could have turned catastrophic. It took four weeks for the FISH to come back with a negative result. The whole time, Barry kept thinking he would be that one-in-a-million case report. He thought the doctor's words spelled doom, when they were really a false positive. In reality, the final word was to the contrary. The events of that day left Dr. K. speechless.

5
IT TAKES A VILLAGE

As hard as it was to get through the second round of induction chemo, Barry made it. Mentally, he was anxious to the point of paranoia. Physically, his body had been to hell and back, his bone marrow completely depleted and recovered—twice. He'd been through numerous infections that required multiple courses of antibiotics and antifungal agents. And yet, despite having spent months face-to-face with his mortality, Barry had to get back to his normal life.

By that point, Barry had been through two rounds of induction chemo at Montefiore and a third at Memorial Sloan Kettering. We were fortunate to have transferred his care to Dr. V. for the third aggressive round and subsequent consolidation chemo, which is a step down in intensity from the induction phase, but nonetheless a knockout punch to the patient who was already pretty banged up.

He didn't feel normal; how could he? There was his appearance. His hair had fallen out, but he had the most chemo-resistant hair; as soon as it was gone, it would regrow. He made a joke out of it. If you asked him,

Daniel S. Mishkin, M.D.

"Would you rather be bald for the rest of your life, or have leukemia and get chemo, knowing the hair will regrow?" he would jokingly opt for the leukemia, in his darkly humorous way. He liked that his hair grew back so quickly. It made it easier to hide his condition—sometimes.

Around this time, he was in a restaurant in Montreal when two guys came over to him and asked, "Are you Barry Mishkin?"

"Yes, I am," he replied.

They weren't from Montreal; they were from the New York area. They had approached Barry because they wanted to tell him they had heard about him through friends, and they'd been following his care. They just wanted to show him their support. They wished him the best of luck and assured him that he should continue to fight.

Now, in Montreal, our family knows a lot of people. But these people were visiting from New York! There was a huge global community following Barry. It was truly encouraging to see how many strangers—really, friends of friends—stepped in to do whatever they could. To this day, I honestly have no idea how many people were involved in caring for our family. There were so many individuals who brought meals, made calls, and so much more to try to make our lives a little easier. I was amazed by the people who would ring the doorbell, leave food, and walk away so that we wouldn't feel beholden to them. Their help came from a place of pure altruism.

I remember a time later on, after Barry had died, when my wife and I were living on Manhattan's Upper West Side. Another couple moved into the same apartment building as us, and we were just getting to know them when he said, "I recognize your name, but I can't remember from where." Then it all came together: he had heard about my family because of the targeted blood donation drives we'd run throughout the area when Barry was sick. My new neighbor's sister had gotten the day off from work

The Other Side of the Bed

in exchange for donating blood for my brother. Her boss had been one of many people in the community who wanted to help in an altruistic way. Everyone wanted to do something—even my new neighbor's sister, someone Barry would never meet.

Targeted blood donations were an important part of how we brought the community into Barry's fight. People who were eager to help could feel like they were doing something, and it was something *very* important. Blood products can carry a risk of infection. No matter what you do to test blood, there's always a small risk of it containing HIV or hepatitis C. We've certainly come a long way in terms of testing blood. Today, the risk of developing HIV from blood donations collected and provided by the Red Cross is extremely low.

Because Barry's bone marrow was knocked out from the chemo, he needed a lot of transfusions, and with each one came the risk of infection. We were concerned, so we organized our own blood drives for targeted donations. Targeted blood donations are collected for a specific individual, not for the blood bank as a whole. If I gave specifically for my brother, it was ideal because I was tested, I was clean, and therefore it was the lowest-risk blood donation he could get.

Certain rules apply. Donors can't give too frequently, because then they could deplete their own blood supply. But people we knew told other people they knew, and pretty soon, it became contagious. People we'd never met were giving targeted blood donations for my brother. Just like my new neighbor's sister and her workplace, some businesses actually offered their employees a day off in exchange for their donation. People wanted to help in whatever way they could.

I found myself being both a helper and one who needed help. After one of Barry's chemo rounds, I was back in Montreal for work when suddenly, I

Daniel S. Mishkin, M.D.

got a call. Barry had an infection and he was being readmitted. I'd only been back for two days, and I'd been working nonstop. There was no way I could drive myself down to New York, but I had to get there. Then I ran into an acquaintance, another doctor in my program. I told him what was going on, that I couldn't get a flight, and that I had to get there.

"I'll drive you down," he said.

He had a few days off and was planning to just hang around Montreal. He said he had an uncle he wanted to visit in New York, and he'd be happy to go. He was a lifesaver. We weren't good friends at the time, but we became really close. He's still one of my best friends to this day. In that situation, what I needed was someone to step in and do something for me that I couldn't do for myself. I didn't know how to ask, but he knew how to offer, and I could accept. That's teamwork.

After transferring his care, Barry's medical team decided to give him another induction dose of chemotherapy to address possible lost ground with the original protocol. The complicated rounds of chemotherapy continued but there was a perceived light at the end of the tunnel. We were now trying to look beyond the next week or just the next round of treatment. We were hopeful of a possible life for Barry after this diagnosis and treatment.

Barry had family and friends on his team, working to make his life as easy as possible. Yet for a sick person, there's tough emotional territory to navigate, much of which healthy people can't understand. Toward the end of his consolidation chemo, when he was still having inpatient admissions for chemotherapy, Barry met another cancer patient, another father around his age, who was also living in Riverdale, New York. This man had lymphoma and was going through some of the same treatments. He and Barry became very friendly.

When they met, both men were inpatients and both were going through a very hard time. They had a lot in common; they were both what's called *neutropenic*, which meant that their white blood cell count was low. In that situation, you need to have reduced physical contact with others to prevent infection. You can't shake hands. You have to wear a mask. If a visitor comes into the room, the person must wear a gown and so on.

Meeting under these circumstances, it's understandable that my brother and this other man would form a bond. They remained friendly after chemo thanks to the fact that they lived in the same area. There is definitely something comforting in being around people who are going through the same things. Here was someone with whom Barry could speak openly about what he was going through.

Both men were struggling with guilt and fear about their families' futures. Barry was terrified that he wouldn't be able to be there for his wife and son. Sari and Jason meant everything to him. Jason was one month old when Barry got sick. Sari was completely consumed by caring for him, as is any mother of a newborn. Now that I have three daughters, I have some understanding of what she must have been going through. At the time, I didn't understand how difficult it is to care for a newborn, never mind dealing with her husband's critical diagnosis and my family now suddenly hovering around.

During his initial diagnosis and treatment, Barry felt like he'd been ripped away from his family. When he was at Montefiore receiving induction chemo, he was confined to the hospital. He couldn't be with the family for whom he was fighting so hard to stay alive. He used to tell friends, "Don't worry about me, there's not much you can do. Take care of Sari and Jason."

He also kept imagining the worst-case scenario: that he would die while his son was still a baby. He kept saying, "It's smarter for me not to be around him so he doesn't feel the pain of losing me."

Daniel S. Mishkin, M.D.

That was hard to hear my brother say, but it was also realistic. Jason couldn't visit much. He couldn't come to the oncology floor of the hospital because of the risk of infection. There are so many immune-suppressed patients, and a seemingly mild cold or virus that an infant carries can devastate a cancer patient. Over the years, when Jason subsequently came to visit the hospital, Barry would go downstairs to the lobby or cafeteria to see him. Barry was in and out of the hospital for two years, so by the end of that, Jason was talking. Once, I remember, he asked his father, "Where do you sleep in the hospital?" As many times as he'd been there to visit, I don't think Jason had ever seen a bed or an inpatient room.

Fortunately, when he was working part-time in the hospital during maintenance chemo, Barry had many afternoons to be with his son. Jason was young then, and I can only hope he has some recollection of those times. I know this was a real highlight for Barry. He had a beautiful and healthy son, and he was so proud of his family. This made it even harder to face the fact that he might soon be ripped from their lives. It helped to have a friend with whom to discuss their shared situation.

A few months after they became friends, the other man's disease suddenly relapsed. He was readmitted. At the time, my brother was in remission, at home. He went to the hospital to visit his friend. Suddenly, my brother was someone else's support.

When my brother first walked into the hospital, he told me it was almost like taking a victory lap. *He was coming in to see someone else.* He wasn't there for an appointment; he was just going to visit a friend who was sick, but deep down, he was extremely nervous. When he saw his friend, however, he found him extremely weak as a result of the medications he was taking.

After seeing him, Barry couldn't take his mind away from his friend's struggle and their shared illness. He found no comfort in anything. It was deeply depressing, because he knew that what was happening to his friend could easily happen to him. He could've been the one in the bed. He was seeing it from the other side, and it was just devastating. At first, I thought, this is great. He's got a support group. Less stress on me and the others. Let him drive this guy crazy. However, once his friend got sick again, it became so much worse.

Soon after, Barry's friend died. My brother fell apart. For a few months, things had been going well. Barry had been looking at his treatment in terms of linear milestones he was moving toward: Get through this treatment, get to the end of the next maintenance chemo, get to that five-year remission mark. But Barry's friend's death threw those rose-tinted plans into the harsh light of reality. It destroyed his morale.

Barry asked me, "Have you ever lost somebody you've spoken to every single day? You go from that to suddenly, the next day, they're gone."

Before long, I knew what that felt like. When he asked me, I knew I would not be able to handle it, no matter how much time and preparation I had.

Barry's grief caused him to withdraw from everyone. He didn't want to be a support to anyone else anymore, and he couldn't even teach medical students any longer. He just withdrew. Luckily, I was coming to New York to start my fellowship soon, the same fellowship program that my brother had started in during the early phase of his disease.

"I can help you," I said. "You don't have to feel like you're a burden on other people. Together, we can do more than another two individuals."

From the medical practice we dreamed of to covering for him at work, that was something positive for him. I wanted to be there and keep him moving forward. To be honest, though, I was really scared.

6
WHAT DOES REMISSION REALLY MEAN?

There were plenty of complications to come. At this point in Barry's treatment, he was technically "cancer-free." Finally, he was on maintenance chemo, which he would need for at least two years if everything went as well as it possibly could. Barry's maintenance chemo was an outpatient regimen. He didn't have to be in the hospital, but he still felt tired, and he needed periodic blood tests. In theory, if he was strong enough, he could go back to work.

Barry's blood work didn't show any signs of cancer, but that was because of the maintenance regimen. We were all waiting on edge. Any second, the other shoe could drop, and the cancer could return.

Because he was out of the hospital and able to return to some parts of his normal life, Barry would run into people all the time who would ask him, "How are you?"

If he said, "I'm cancer-free," that would be true, but it would also be misleading to someone who doesn't know the medicine. At first, he would tell people, "I'm cancer-free," then hear their elation and have to explain

Daniel S. Mishkin, M.D.

the rest of the chemo regimen. Many of them would think his treatment was done—the cancer, defeated and never to be an issue again. The intricacies of cancer treatment make the explanations difficult. In the course of polite conversation, Barry would have to get into details he didn't really want to discuss.

Barry got to a point where he would say, "I'm doing well. Things are going as planned." Nevertheless, people would reply, "Well, what does that mean? I heard you're cancer-free. Are you cancer-free?" People meant well, but it was exhausting for him. Remarkably, these conversations about my brother and his illness were all taking place prior to the popularization of e-mail and social media. Nevertheless, because people are so intimately connected, the community knew everything in an instant. It was a double-edged sword; it was a nice to have all the support, but it was also tiring because we were constantly answering the same questions. Barry was left with little privacy, adding further psychological strain.

In his cancer-free state, Barry did, in fact, return to work. It was a struggle. There were always complications. The complications didn't necessarily have to do with Barry's current state of health; sometimes, they were emotional. Barry was still in a critical state of health. He was very conscious about the way he was spending his precious time. For example, one Friday morning, he had a liver clinic that he had to work—and felt obliged to do so—but he wanted to come home to Montreal for an event on Friday night. So the question was, how could he get out of that Friday-morning clinic?

Barry's colleagues had been covering for him while he was sick. As he weighed whether or not to ask one for a favor, he was sure they would think, *What are you talking about? You've taken off so much time and we've picked up so much slack; we need you!* He didn't want to burden them, and he didn't want to feel even more indebted to anyone else, but at the same time, he had leukemia. He didn't know how much time he had left. He felt like he had to make it work and get away somehow. These difficult decisions were part of his everyday reality.

We talked about this fine line all the time.

I told him, "Talk to those guys. You have cancer; you're allowed to be selfish. Do whatever you need to do. Just get out of that Friday-morning clinic."

Barry did not share my perspective. He was such a team player, and he really wanted to put in as many hours as he could. He was always thinking about how his actions affected others. He only took time off when things were extreme, when he really needed to. With his anxious nature, he was always aware that the day would come when he would be unable to work at all. In the meantime, he wanted to stay in everyone's good graces.

As he dealt with the daily negotiations, Barry was also inspired to find some greater value in his suffering. That was how the idea for this book first came about: he kept telling me that his struggle had to somehow give meaning to others.

The first result of that impulse came in Barry's teaching. Once, working with medical students, he taught them by using some of the details of his own hospital admission. It definitely hit home for them. Barry saw how much they were affected emotionally by hearing his story. He was their teacher, but he was also in the middle of an incredible fight for his life. They were amazed by his candor and his willingness to share his experience. Barry could see what a difference it made to tell his personal story. He'd felt so wrapped up in his suffering, but telling his story showed him that something positive could come out of this experience. Now that he has passed, I am writing this book to create a positive teaching experience from my brother's memory. Ultimately, I am doing this for him.

Daniel S. Mishkin, M.D.

When Barry returned to work, he should have been a full-time gastroenterology fellow, but in his physical state, he couldn't handle the workload. One of the chemo's side effects was peripheral neuropathy: he couldn't feel his fingers. Gastroenterology is a very procedure-heavy field. You can't do procedures without sensation in your fingers. It was endlessly frustrating for him, but he never let himself be defeated. He kept on saying, "It's going to be OK." He knew he had to keep going for his son. He told me, "If this is what I have to live through in order to be able to survive and be here for my son, Jason, then I'm willing to do it." He kept repeating that like a mantra; he had to be there for his wife and son, Sari and Jason.

His focus on Jason helped him to work through the anger and frustration he felt. Barry was angry about losing his ability to practice independently. He never really spoke about it; I knew because I knew him well enough. Asking about it would have been like pouring salt in a wound.

Barry's peripheral neuropathy was another push for me to go into the field of gastroenterology (GI). At first, I wanted to go into cardiology. I would have been happy doing anything in medicine, but cardiology was my first choice. Cardiology and GI are both procedure-oriented internal-medicine subspecialties, which would allow me to continually learn and try to develop new technologies. Each of these fields provides great opportunities in addition to all the aspects of medicine that I enjoy.

Once Barry knew that he couldn't perform procedures any more, my decision was clear: I would go into GI. We would practice together; he could handle the liver and office-based practice, while I took care of the procedures. We would each be happy, and we'd get the job done as a team.

I didn't see GI as a compromise. My brother and I were so very close. I knew that without me, he would not have been able to continue in medicine at the capacity he had hoped for. I didn't want to see that happen.

Together, we would be even greater than the sum of our two individual parts. The dream of practicing together gave us something positive to focus on for the future, and it was something we talked about regularly. You can't look back at what might have been; you have to focus on the way forward.

When Barry returned to work, he found what he could do well. There's dignity in all work—taking blood pressure, scrubbing floors, etc. Barry saw a niche for himself in educating young doctors, as well as seeing patients in the ambulatory clinics. Even if Barry's health couldn't handle the crazy hours of being on service or performing procedures, he worked collaboratively with his co-fellows to contribute to the team. The world needs doctors who can teach. Barry's personal experience as a patient provided insight to doctors steeped in the technical side of medicine. His experience also allowed him to understand complicated practice. His skills would've been ideal for an office practice. He was more understanding of chronic patients' needs, of the ways that their disease was affecting them. The fact is, Montefiore was really good to Barry, despite his having transferred his care to another hospital. People there understood his situation and made exceptions so that he could continue to work. They *never* questioned or judged him.

Much later, I got word of a meeting that took place at Montefiore not long after he got sick. The administrators in charge called in all the attending physicians. They laid out the situation: They had enough money and space for three fellows. Given Barry's situation, they had the option to make a determination that one of those fellows, Barry, would have to drop out. If so, they could replace him. At this time, though, most of the high-caliber candidates had likely committed to other programs. Montefiore could look for another doctor who would essentially be an extra body, or they could leave Barry on the payroll—not to mention, on the insurance.

Daniel S. Mishkin, M.D.

Then, if and when he got better, he could come back. They knew his work ethic. They loved him and knew that he would try to give them as much as he could.

While I have never heard the specifics of what went on in that meeting, I know the end result was that Barry stayed. I understand that one person had made a case that keeping him on was the only humane option. Ultimately, it was a show of respect for Barry and his young family. I knew that I needed to try to repay the team at Montefiore, and I had a plan.

As Barry tried to hold on to his career, I focused on supporting him. In October 2000, a year and a half after he was first diagnosed, it was time for me to apply for GI fellowships. With my brother in the forefront of my mind, I applied to only two places: Montefiore Hospital and another New York hospital with a stellar reputation and highly competitive program. I had met some of the people at Montefiore; they knew me as Barry's little brother who might be interested in GI. But I hadn't been in their hospital since the previous June. Back then, my presence in the hospital was as a sick patient's family member, not a medical student or resident. I knew who they were, but they didn't really know me. They hadn't seen my résumé or references before I applied.

However, a few years prior, I'd had a professional encounter with one of the attending gastroenterologists. I was in New York visiting Barry during his internship at Montefiore. Because I was a medical student, I got to tag along on rounds. Dr. L. was the attending in charge. He's got an encyclopedic mind; to this day, he's one of the smartest people I've ever met. He asked a question about a very rare condition. It was a situation that was likely taught once in medical school, then forgotten.

That kind of detail is my specialty, so I knew the answer. Barry immediately shot me a look that told me to be quiet, but Dr. L. recognized by my grin that I'd had a lightbulb go on in my head, so he asked me what I thought. I looked at my brother to ask, "Can I answer?" only to see him shake his head. Who would want to be upstaged at work by his little brother?

Then, Dr. L. said, "Go ahead; if you know the answer, tell me."

I said, "Leber's hereditary optic neuropathy."

We made an instant connection, and later he pulled me aside. We talked about my interests and was curious to get to know me better. This felt like a dream come true.

Years later, when I was invited for my fellowship interviews at Montefiore, one of the interviewers asked, "Is this your first choice?"

My immediate reply was "yes."

Toward the end of the interview, the chief of the department, Dr. N., turned to me.

"I'm going to ask you one question, and the position may be dependent on it: If your brother gets sick, are you going to take time off?"

There are certain questions that you're never allowed to ask in interviews, such as "Are you pregnant?" or "Are you planning to become pregnant during the course of your training?" Dr. N.'s question was completely inappropriate, but he deserved to know. I also knew that there was a debt to repay. I wouldn't lie.

So, without any hesitation, I replied, "If my brother is sick, I will take care of him. I've done it up until now, and I will repay everyone who helped me to do that. That's what I've done in Montreal, and they haven't had a problem with it. I'll be honest with you. I missed a lot of time in Montreal. I paid it back in spades, but—"

Dr. N. interrupted me.

"Let me give you the problem with that answer," he began. "Right now, we have three fellows per year for three years, so we have nine fellows. When you will be starting as a first year, in theory, your brother will be a third-year

Daniel S. Mishkin, M.D.

fellow. If he gets sick, and both of you are unavailable, we're down to seven. We can't function like that. Unless you guarantee that you're going to be able to work, we can't do this. Think about it."

"There's nothing to think about," I said. "I appreciate the opportunity. Thank you very much." I shook his hand and walked out. *That's that*, I thought. I was sure I wouldn't get an offer from them.

I had my interview with the other site the following day. They reviewed my résumé, we navigated the whole process, and I thought it went well—yet I finished the day feeling very nervous. With all of Barry's medical issues and catching up on call and coverage requirements back in Montreal, I hadn't applied to many programs. I felt I was a strong candidate, and I hoped that Montefiore would receive me well. Suddenly, I realized that they didn't necessarily see it the same way. I needed to be in New York. I didn't want to delay my fellowship from starting.

Even though there was an official time at which hospitals were supposed to make offers, many contracts were signed before then. The stronger candidates were often taken earlier, as there was no match for medical subspecialties at this time. If you thought you had a great fit, you signed them on the spot.

After the interviews, I went back to Montreal. That Sunday night, I got a call from the second site at which I'd interviewed. They were offering me a spot in their program.

I said, "OK. Thank you very much."

The doctor replied, "So, you're accepting?"

"Can I have until tomorrow?" I asked.

"You've got to be joking," he said. "No one turns us down."

The program was probably the most desired in the city at the time, and it was just assumed that that was where I wanted to go. Part of me really *did* want to go there. This would have been a real feather in my cap.

Nevertheless, I told him that I needed one day to get back to him. "Can you give me that?"

I called Montefiore and explained what happened.

"I'll send you a contract right now," said the man who, just a few days before, had told me that my commitment to caring for my brother was an issue. In some ways, I was pressuring him into taking me into the program, but that was what I really wanted. I wanted to be with my brother, and I knew that it was a very strong program. I also knew that they had their personal priorities straight. They had been so good to Barry. It was a win-win situation.

The primary reason I wanted to be at Montefiore was because Barry was there, and the people there knew him—they knew what he had been through. While a workplace might try to be understanding when an employee is called to tend to a sick family member, it's hard. At Montefiore, because they all knew and cared for my brother, it was much easier; he was one of their own.

If I had accepted the other program's offer, it would have been impossible to take off more time if Barry got sick again, something for which I needed to prepare. It was much less of a family-type environment. Regardless, I never would have believed that a medical fellow could pull off what I did. Who would have thought that I would have been able to be with my brother in another city as much as I was during my training, and not fall behind? I still wonder how it all happened, and I know I had a lot of help from my peers and mentors along the way, yet I still made sure to meet all the residency's requirements.

To this day, I still run into the person who made me the offer from the other fellowship site. When I run into him at conferences—all the time—he says, "Hey, it's the only person who ever turned us down!"

I was desperate to help my brother, and I tried my best to be there for him as much as I could. At times, that meant going above and beyond in

Daniel S. Mishkin, M.D.

my own medical studies to advance my knowledge and experience so that I could help out wherever I was needed. There was one particular opportunity, which occurred about two years after Barry got sick and just before I moved to New York for my fellowship, that gave me the chance to do that.

As I've mentioned before, in Canada, medical students and residents do much more during their training with less supervision. In the United States, everything is supervised much more rigorously. There are pros and cons to both systems. In March of 2001, I was finishing up my residency in Montreal and had already accepted the GI fellowship position at Montefiore. I would be moving to New York to start my fellowship that July. Then one day, I got a call from the GI department in the hospital where I was working in Montreal.

The attending on the other end of the line said, "The GI fellow is sick. Can you cover as the GI fellow for two weeks?"

I was scheduled to be working in the intensive care unit during that time. They offered me two fewer weeks of ICU time if I would help them out as a GI fellow. Now, I wasn't trained to be a GI fellow, but they knew I was interested and was going to begin a GI fellowship in three months' time. I had done rotations with the attending physicians in that field, and those doctors knew me.

They needed someone who could take on the responsibility of doing the work but who also had a knowledge base sufficient to run the service with an attending's supervision. I could do what was necessary to run the day-to-day activities with experienced doctors keeping an eye on me.

It sounded ideal, so I said, "Absolutely."

For those two weeks, the attending physicians appreciated my eagerness and willingness to learn, which motivated them to teach me even more. To my surprise, they began to allow me to perform procedures such as endoscopy. Here I was, a third-year resident, operating a colonoscope or a gastroscope on actual patients. I wasn't great at it; it can take months or years to get great, but it really helped me to get a feel for the basics, and since the attending was present, none of the patients were at an increased risk of harm. It was an important two weeks for me to start understanding how to manipulate complex technology and it helped build my confidence.

When I arrived in New York, I had already surpassed the beginner stage. So here I was, a week or two into my GI fellowship, operating an endoscope. One of the GI attendings was supervising, watching over my shoulder.

He said, "Wow, this is very impressive. How do you know how to do this?"

As a fellow, it's rare to get such praise from an attending. Barry was also in the room. I could feel him beaming with pride, so happy to see me working hard and doing well. He hated seeing me struggle. In one type of rounds, we fellows would present cases to the supervising doctors. If I got a question wrong and my brother was there, you could tell it hurt him much more than it hurt me. I was OK with making mistakes. It still hurt, of course, but if I knew everything, I wouldn't need to be trained. I had enough confidence in myself to believe that I was right more often than I was wrong. If I missed a question, I wouldn't necessarily remember it. My brother always would.

I'm so grateful to have that memory of working side by side with Barry. I loved it—but working with my brother did provoke one unexpected reaction from a supervising doctor. Once, when we were in a procedure together, I was scoping, and the attending in the room started yelling at me. I was in the middle of the procedure, with the patient anaesthetized in front of me. The doctor went on to insult me for the next fifteen minutes.

Daniel S. Mishkin, M.D.

He thought he was teaching me a lesson to prevent me from becoming arrogant. He seemed to think that if he didn't break me down, even in front of my brother, I'd never succeed in the field.

My brother walked out sometime in the middle of the attending's tirade. I later found out that he'd gone somewhere and cried. He was devastated that he couldn't stand up to the attending, especially when I was not doing anything significantly wrong. He couldn't jump in. Whether it was on the hockey rink or anywhere else, he had always been my protector. But here, in his own hospital, he couldn't defend me. And that bothered him.

After he yelled at me, the attending pulled me aside.

"Listen," he began, "you need to learn a few things."

"OK," I said.

I was respectful and quiet. I felt chewed up inside from being yelled at, but I did not react. Later that night, I wanted to cry, but at this point in my medical training, I was sort of used to it. The method is a bit old school and less prevalent now; however, I can see how it became part of the culture. When you're yelled at and beaten down, it can help build you up in some ways. You end up working *much* harder the next time. I don't agree with the practice, but I got used to it.

The purpose of breaking people down is to get them to recognize that they don't understand everything. As doctors, we have to be willing to be humbled. You can't get too cocky; the constant pressure made me more levelheaded about my abilities. If you come in thinking you know everything, you're never going to learn enough to actually succeed. The more experienced doctors sometimes use intimidation to get young doctors to listen. I thought the attending was trying to show me that I still had a lot to learn. He was impressing on me a hierarchy of experience; maybe it made sense in the context.

But then he said, "Listen, you did a good job, but I'm going to make sure that your brother knows that he is the better Mishkin of the two of you."

My jaw dropped. He was yelling at me in front of my brother just to make my brother feel *better?* What kind of world was this? I still don't understand what happened that day, and I probably never will.

I couldn't say anything, but I felt like I wanted to explode. At the same time, I knew that my brother would be waiting to talk to me after I got out of the procedure room. Would I tell him what this guy had said to me? Or would I brush it off? Afterward, Barry came to me, devastated.

I told him, "It was nothing."

He shook his head and said, "I couldn't defend you. I couldn't be there for you. I couldn't say anything."

The attending's tactic accomplished the exact opposite of what was supposed to happen. I've seen the medical hierarchy teach people well, but I've also seen hospital politics backfire more times than I can count. On my first day working on the wards as a first-year resident, when I was still in Montreal, a patient started to hemorrhage with a large amount of bright-red blood passed per rectum and was imminently about to become unstable.

I turned to the person at the desk and asked, "Are you the secretary?"

"No," she replied.

I said, "I don't care *who* you are; call a code!"

She wouldn't do it. Why? Because I'd called her a secretary, when her job title was unit coordinator. I do my best to refer to everyone by the right title, but in a life-or-death situation, you have to leave your ego at the door! You have to respond and do what you're called upon to do. Someone else ended up calling the code, and the patient's life was saved, but for months, this person gave me grief. The patient developed a massive bleed from an

Daniel S. Mishkin, M.D.

aortoenteric fistula, which is an abnormal connection between the aorta and the intestinal tract. In this case, the graft repair had become infected with *E. coli* bacteremia six months after an abdominal aortic aneurysm repair; the source of *E. coli* bacteremia had been missed when he was admitted two days beforehand. The aorta was pumping blood directly into the small intestine and he was in trouble. The patient was immediately taken to the operating room and ultimately did very well. I, on the other hand, was not in a good place, as the unit coordinator wouldn't talk to me and tried to make my life on the wards very difficult. Finally, six months later, she started being nice to me when other people told her to knock it off. She was just trying to control a situation, but the timing was wrong. A patient could have died.

In the early days of my fellowship, I was extremely motivated. I was excited to be at Montefiore and to give back to the place that had treated my brother so well. I was also a GI fellow, working crazy hours and hardly getting any time off.

It wasn't all bad. The world works in mysterious ways. Once, at the end of a long day, I was getting ready to leave the hospital. It was around 6:30 p.m. I finished rounding, did all my paperwork, and began to head out the door.

Then, one of the attendings approached me and said, "I need you to see one more patient."

Immediately, I thought, *Why can't you do it? Can't this wait for tomorrow?* Of course, I answered my own questions and proceeded to see the patient.

I went back upstairs to see the patient, knowing he was really sick and this could take some time. *Not the end of the world,* I thought. I was tired, but he needed my help. I tracked the patient down in the dialysis unit, and found an acutely ill man writhing in pain. Without a doubt, he needed surgery. I didn't know exactly what it was, but it was clear the patient was in severe abdominal distress.

I tried to reach the attending who had assigned me to this patient, but he was unavailable. So, I wrote up the consult and called the surgical team to come see the patient. I had met the surgical fellow before.

When he walked in, he said, "You know, you really screwed me."

"What?" I asked, surprised.

"I had hockey tickets tonight. My buddy's waiting for me at Madison Square Garden. I have both tickets."

The surgeon was from Toronto, and the Maple Leafs were playing the Rangers that night. With this emergency surgery, he knew there was no way he'd make it to the game—and without one of the tickets, both of which the surgeon had, neither would his friend.

"Hey, this is perfect!" I said.

I offered to take the tickets, meet his friend at the game, and enjoy the hockey for him. It wasn't the end of the world for the surgeon, and I was badly in need of a night out. I got to go watch my favorite sport, blow off some steam, and help out another guy I'd never met before.

At the beginning of my fellowship, I was on call a lot. I was also trying to spend as much time as possible with my brother. I was living in a new city, wanting to make new friends, and needing to preserve my own mental sanity as well as a long-distance relationship with my girlfriend of two years' time.

I was eager to show my appreciation for Barry's colleagues. They had worked so hard to pick up the work he couldn't do, and they were feeling burned out. They were frustrated with him and with the situation. I probably would have felt the same way. There's only so long that you can hear the same story about a person's illness before you become desensitized to the real facts of it. It's just human nature.

Daniel S. Mishkin, M.D.

If you know anyone with chronic illness, whether it's rheumatoid arthritis, or Crohn's disease, or debilitating psoriasis—every time you see him, do you ask him how he's doing? Do you bring it up? At the beginning, or during hard times, it's more in the forefront of your mind. It's easier to be there for that person. But after some time has passed, the desire to help sort of recedes. Usually, the person who is sick is trying to protect his privacy and dignity, and the community begins to stop asking. You forget.

What's the right way to support someone with chronic illness? There's obviously no one correct thing to do; every patient is different. As a doctor, I've learned that many times, patients know more about their own disease than doctors do.

There were times when Barry wanted to hide his illness, and there were times when he wanted to ask his colleagues to give him a break. He sometimes wished he could say, "Leave me alone; I'm doing my best." But he was a really good guy and he never resorted to pushing people away in self-defense.

As a patient, it was very hard for Barry to be known by his diagnosis. Every time he went into the emergency room or saw a doctor, he felt like he was reduced to one dimension: his disease. In medicine, that's how doctors refer to patients, as in, "This is a thirty-one-year-old male with a diagnosis of acute lymphocytic leukemia who was in his usual state of health until . . ." He would always be that person, always known by his diagnosis. He had a hard time with that.

Barry's illness became a visible part of him. As part of the chemo treatment delivered at the cancer hospital, Barry had an Ommaya reservoir implanted in his scalp. An Ommaya reservoir is a pouch on the top of the head that can be injected with medicine that is delivered directly into the fluid that surrounds the brain. On a patient with a bald head, it's hard to miss. When one has a full head of hair, it can be camouflaged, but it is always visible close-up. In my office, I keep a picture of my brother at my wedding, on March 7, 2002, more than a year after the insertion. In that photo, he has a full head of hair. You would never know that he was sick, or that he had an Ommaya reservoir. He passed away exactly five months later, to the day. But if he had been receiving chemo and his hair had fallen out, or if he had shaved it off, this bump would've been quite obvious.

At the time, he tried to deal by making jokes. He would say that he loved having a hole in his head. Still, it was always clear that he hated being known by his disease. He analyzed everything about his interactions, especially people's gazes. He used to say, "I can always tell where people are looking. Are they looking at my head, are they looking at my eyes, or are they not even looking at my face? When people tilt their heads to the side, I can tell they don't see me as a regular person; they see me as a cancer patient."

He knew it would never be any different. Even if he beat the illness, he would be known by his friends and community as a survivor, defined by the disease.

7
NOT AGAIN

Dealing with Relapse

After starting a fellowship in the same city and the same program as my brother, I would've thought that it would have been easier for me to be there for him. One day, at the end of July 2001, I got a phone call.

"Barry's in trouble," the caller said.

Suddenly, Barry had developed a heart arrhythmia. I had to go to him immediately. I was working at another hospital, about a fifteen-minute drive away, in the same area of the Bronx. We didn't know it at the time, but that's when everything started to go downhill.

Whenever you go into a hospital as an employee, there are certain things you need to know. As a resident or an attending, you need to know how to live in a hospital. It can be as simple as navigating the bathrooms or finding the food storage so you can eat in the middle of the night. That July, I had barely found the bathrooms in the hospital where I was working when I got the phone call. I turned to my colleagues and told them what was happening.

Daniel S. Mishkin, M.D.

They said, "Go. Go. Just be with Barry."

I was gone. I ran to the stairwell, because I knew the elevator would take too long. I had to get to the parking lot behind the hospital so I could make the short drive from where I was to where my brother was in crisis.

The stairwell, however, was not the best way to get there. I remember that somewhere along the way, I passed a sign that read, "NO EXIT," but I kept going anyway. I opened the door at the end of the stairwell, stepped out, and it latched behind me. I was standing at the edge of a sheer drop into a construction ditch. It was like a scene from a James Bond movie, except I, the hapless protagonist in khakis and a tie, definitely could not jump the ditch. I turned around and started banging on the door hoping someone would come to my rescue. I realized that I had missed the previous signs. No one else would be dumb enough to come near that door. After a minute or so of that, I thought, *What the hell? My brother needs me! I'll do anything! I'll summon my superhuman strength, and jump!*

I didn't make it far. I fell into the ditch and just ran. I fell flat on my face. After some time, I was able to crawl out of the ditch, but I was definitely worse for the wear. When I finally got to the hospital, I looked worse than my brother did. My khakis were caked in mud, and my face was dripping with sweat. I was out of breath and exhausted. I had no idea what was going on.

Barry was in atrial fibrillation, with a very rapid and irregular pulse rate. The doctors ended up correcting it with medication, but things were not right, and they ended up doing a variety of testing. Barry knew something was really, really wrong. It was the end of July. It took about three months for us to confirm that even though he was on maintenance chemo, the leukemia was causing trouble again.

The doctors struggled to figure out what exactly was going on with Barry's health. I worked pretty much all the time, and when I wasn't working, I spent time with Barry and his family. Whether we were at the hospital for work or at his home, I saw him nearly every day. It was a relief to be in New York and not be going back and forth from Montreal. Still, there was plenty of personal sacrifice. A few years beforehand, in Montreal, I had begun dating Stef. When I moved down to New York for my fellowship, she and I continued dating, long distance. She would come down to New York every other weekend to spend time with me. I couldn't really take time away, so she did the work of traveling back and forth so we could be together. I am still so grateful to her for that. She was a huge support for the whole family as we went through the next stage of Barry's illness.

Once we knew that Barry's cancer was back, we knew the treatments he'd gone through before hadn't worked. The chemo had kept the disease at bay for a time, but we couldn't try the same tactic again. Actually, it was likely that Barry had developed a second leukemia due to the toxicity of the aggressive chemo. It was crazy to think that at the beginning, we needed stronger medications, but in the end, it was the aggressive chemo that likely led to a second leukemia. A bone marrow transplant became his only option.

Barry began to feel even more social anxiety when we found out that neither my sister nor I were a bone marrow match for him. You see, a bone marrow transplant can cure some kinds of leukemia. When he first got sick, I got tested and found out that I was not a match for him. We looked so much alike. People used to see us in different situations and mix us up, even though side by side, we were easy to tell apart. After he passed away, people who didn't know he had died would approach me assuming that I was him.

Daniel S. Mishkin, M.D.

One friend's mother had Alzheimer's disease and thought I was Barry for the last years of her life; I never corrected her.

I felt guilty that I couldn't provide Barry with a transplant that could save him. The highest likelihood of finding a donor who is most like the patient is within the patient's own family. Having to explore outside of our family, we were looking for a needle in a haystack. In those days, there was not a great chance of finding a match through a bone marrow registry. We needed to do a bone marrow registration drive. Donating bone marrow was much more complex than donating blood. It would have been the perfect time to do the drives when Barry first got sick because it takes time to test and to enroll people.

I went to him and said, "We have to do a bone marrow drive," and he refused.

While the bone marrow transplant would be a last resort if the chemo did not take care of the leukemia, we pushed to no avail to try and prepare for a rainy day that might come.

Finally, in September 2001, about two and a half years after his diagnosis, I said, "We're doing this."

He still begged me not to. At this point, there was no choice, as his disease had taken a turn for the worse.

To donate bone marrow, people first have to be tested and enrolled in the registry. Then, if a patient is a match for a donor in the registry, the next steps can be taken for harvest and transplant.

At that point, I had only been in New York for a few months, but I'd spent years training in Montreal. My sister and I, along with our family and friends, organized a drive in Montreal that enrolled more than a thousand people in the registry. Héma-Québec, the provincial organization in charge of the bone marrow registry, had never seen anything like it.

Today, a simple cheek swab is enough to add a person to the registry, but back then in Montreal, you had to do blood draws. We had so much support in gathering those thousand blood samples. First, there were the twenty-odd nurses who volunteered to run twelve stations of simultaneous blood draws. Then, there were the people who came in and had their blood taken, waiting in line to enroll. We felt so supported by the community as we organized this monster in less than three weeks' time.

While my family and I poured our energy into signing up people to save lives, Barry was still horrified by the attention. He refused to be there as the sick patient, the poster child. For the Montreal drive, his justification was simple: he lived elsewhere and could not come in.

This first bone marrow drive was so successful that we knew we had to hold another one—this time, in New York. I only had three weeks to fundraise for the event. I turned to the community in which Barry; his wife, Sari; and their baby, Jason, lived. They had gotten to know a lot of people, and his story spread quickly.

One day, I had arranged to meet a man who was a friend of some of Barry's friends. I sat down in his home, and I told him what I was trying to do with the bone marrow drives. I told him how many people we'd signed up in Montreal, and how many we thought we could sign up in New York. One major difference between the cities and their health-care systems was that in Canada, such drives were was covered by socialized health care, whereas in the United States, we had to worry about fundraising to accommodate such a large group and its costs. However, this drive would be somewhat simpler, with only cheek swabs required to test the genetic makeup for a match.

Within fifteen minutes of meeting him, he asked, "How much money do you need?"

Daniel S. Mishkin, M.D.

I ran through the numbers: the cost of each swab kit and testing each sample.

He said, "I'm in. Here's a credit card. Print up flyers. Order food. I'll take care of whatever you need to get a thousand people enrolled—and if you recruit more than that, I'll find a way to take care of that too."

This was a fifteen-minute conversation with someone who simply cared to do the right thing. He knew my brother indirectly, and although he had never spent any real time with him, he opened up his wallet. Once one person said yes, others did too. There was a snowball effect. The money went straight to Gift of Life, the group organizing the bone marrow drives in New York.

That day in Riverdale, we signed up more than two thousand people. I was told it took months to test all the samples we collected that day. It wasn't easy. I was still working full time, so I delegated as much as I could. Two people in Barry's network were in the PR field, and they helped. They made the flyers and got us on the radio. I remember listening to the radio announcers talk about the drive on the various popular radio stations. I had no idea what we were doing; I only knew how to plead for help, and miraculously, things somehow fell into place for the drive.

Barry never showed up to the New York enrollment drive either. People asked why he wasn't there. In their minds, it would be comforting for him to see all the people who showed up to help. Barry didn't see it that way. He didn't want to be known as the cancer patient. That was his choice, and I had to honor it, even if I didn't agree with it.

As a result, I ended up feeling as though *I* were the poster child. Later, that became one of the reasons why I ultimately decided to leave New York. In places where people had known Barry and the bone marrow and blood drives, people would always see me and ask, "How's your brother?" Some people even confused me with him. Then came the awful moment when I'd have to tell them, "He passed away."

"Oh my God," they'd respond. "I donated blood," or "I joined the bone marrow registry," or whatever else. Every time, it was like Barry was dying all over again.

As hard as it is to retell my brother's story, the community support was amazing, and it has extended far beyond Barry's struggle. Thousands of people entered the bone marrow registry at a time when there weren't that many Eastern Europeans in the registry. An even greater number of people have since been saved because my brother raised awareness of the need to enroll people in this program, as dozens of people have now donated bone marrow from the drives we ran. Other people decided to run drives—big ones—in other towns and cities. People just wanted to help.

Barry didn't want people to know about his health, but if he went out with friends and no one said anything about his condition, he would sometimes get annoyed. He could be like a kid who wanted attention. So his mood would go up and down, but for the most part, he just wanted to be seen as normal. He wanted to do more with his life. This is something all patients live with in attempting not to be seen as "the sick one," yet still needing enough support to push forward in the fight.

It was a lengthy process and a difficult procedure. First, the worldwide database would have to find him a suitable match. We had run bone marrow drives to increase the possibility of that, but given the timeline, the process was unlikely to result in any matches. It was more for us, to feel like we were doing something to help, than for him. We enrolled thousands of people, but in comparison to the astronomical need for donors, we barely made a dent in the numbers. If a match were found, they would have to be prepared, and the cells, harvested.

Daniel S. Mishkin, M.D.

Then Barry would need to undergo aggressive chemo to destroy his own bone marrow cells so that the donor cells would have a vacant space to occupy and hopefully grow. During this aggressive chemo, any infection can cause a huge setback. Finally Barry would have to go on antirejection medications to prevent his immune system from rejecting these cells that belonged to someone else. For that reason, a patient needs as close a match as possible to his or her own genetic makeup. Hopefully, Barry's body would see these cells as similar enough to his native cells to allow them to reproduce in his body. The whole process could take months.

From the very beginning of his treatment, Barry was face-to-face with his mortality. With a cancer diagnosis, it was impossible not to be. After his friend died, his concern became an obsession. He was worried about his family. At the time, Barry had been in school for nearly his whole life. He was thirty-one when he got sick, working as a chief resident, with a four-week-old baby. He had done well throughout his training, but in medicine at the time, residents rarely made more than $40,000 a year. Medical school debt and expenses can take a lifetime to pay off. What if he didn't have a lifetime? Barry was wrestling with so many feelings of burdening others. He felt the need to make sure that Sari and Jason were taken care of, that they weren't saddled with his student debt, and that they could live out their lives without worry if he were to pass away. He wanted Jason to grow up healthy and happy. He wanted Sari to remarry if she wanted to. He wanted to make sure that they could thrive without him, as difficult as that might be.

Sometimes, his regret would turn to anger. I hated the spite I heard in those moments, the disease coming to wreak havoc on Barry's emotions as well as his body. In those moments, I learned to listen to my brother as he voiced his greatest fears and regrets. If I didn't listen, who would? He needed to be heard. He needed to feel validated and cared for in mind as well as body. People in terrible situations sometimes have a unique clarity of mind, and he was gaining that clarity while simultaneously losing his mind.

Barry cherished all the time he spent with his son, yet there was so much he missed: milestones, daily events. Of all the things he missed, there was one seemingly small event that hit him particularly hard. One day, Barry had been having a really hard time health-wise, and he and Sari decided to spend some time alone. The rest of us left the hospital. My mom and Stef took care of Jason.

When I got off work that day, I went to the playground where my mom and Stef were with Jason. Just as I arrived, Jason fell off a swing and cut the back of his head; he began bleeding quite profusely. Immediately, I thought of what to do. Barry and Sari were close friends with a couple; the wife was a pediatric ER physician, and the husband was a cardiologist. They lived just two buildings down from the park. I called them, and we rushed over.

At their apartment, the pediatrician cleaned Jason up, stopped the bleeding, and closed the wound. After it was all taken care of, we called Barry and Sari to tell them what had happened. When Barry heard the news, he was livid. It was one of the few times throughout his whole illness that Barry actually yelled at me. He must have felt so powerless.

He shouted, "You're not responsible for my child! You should have called me; you should have let *me* decide where to take him and what to do! You should have taken him to a hospital!"

The event must have provoked Barry's fear that he wouldn't be able to be there for Jason, triggering all the emotional baggage that came with that. We'd only wanted to let Barry and Sari have time alone, to protect them from what seemed like a small childhood event, yet we'd caused another conflict. I kept apologizing, saying I was wrong and that I should have

Daniel S. Mishkin, M.D.

called. Now, with three kids of my own, I feel even worse. I knew he was right then; now, I know even more how right he was. That day still reverberates in my head. I hope he eventually forgave me.

Later on, as Barry thought more about how to connect with his son while he was in the hospital receiving treatment, he decided to make a picture book just for Jason. Barry wrote the book and got a friend to illustrate it. It was filled with the things that Barry and Jason used to do together. One page read, "We woke up in the morning and played trains." The illustrator drew bodies playing with trains, and Barry pasted in photos of his and Jason's heads.

Barry devoted significant time and energy to the picture book because he wanted Jason to have something special and to feel like they were still spending time together while they were apart. It may seem like a small gesture, but it was extremely important for Barry. It was a focus, a productive place where he could channel his energy. It also took his mind off his own struggle. He had to think and write about things other than cancer and medicine. How can you relate suffering to a child? You can't. You can only communicate things that are physical and positive to create a feeling of intimacy and love. He told me, "With this, I'm leaving a legacy for Jason." It was so important for him to create something that Jason would understand and that would convey how much his father loved him, even after he was gone.

One day when I was a second-year resident in Montreal and I was on call in the hospital, I received a page at 2:30 a.m. I was groggy; I'd only been asleep for half an hour. I jolted up and answered the page.

"You've got to get here; a patient is exsanguinating," said the voice on the end of the line.

"Exsanguinating?" I asked. What was he talking about? I'd been awakened in the middle of the night plenty of times for codes, but this was an entirely new one.

The Other Side of the Bed

I ran up to the surgical floor, where the patient was. He was scheduled for surgery the next day for a tumor surrounding his carotid artery. The carotid artery is the major blood vessel going into the brain. He was around seventy years old. His surgery was scheduled for early the next morning, and his wife was staying overnight in the room with him. In the middle of the night, she woke up, felt something wet, and screamed.

There was blood everywhere—on the ceiling, the walls, the floor, and the beds in which both of them had been sleeping. His wife was covered in blood, which was what had awakened her. The tumor had eroded through the artery, and the patient's heart was sending sprays of blood all over the room.

We were told immediately that the patient had an end-of-life directive; he didn't want any heroic measures. But now, here, in the middle of the night, stood his wife covered in blood. Instead of waiting for surgery, she was now mourning her husband's death. It was two thirty in the morning. How would she get home? Should she wake her children, who lived in other cities? There were so many new issues to deal with.

The patient hadn't suffered; he'd been unconscious. But now we had to take care of his widow. She was in shock. We stayed with her for approximately ninety minutes, but there was nothing we could say or do to bring back her husband. She was speechless. We stayed for her emotional, not medical, support. It's part of caring for the whole patient, even though this was the just beginning of the patient's widow's new reality.

I'll never forget one patient whom I met when I was in college, volunteering on the palliative care ward. Early on, I was in this patient's room making small talk and seeing if she needed anything. She was in her usual state of enjoying pleasant conversation when suddenly, she started waving her hands above her head like she was trying to brush something away. She was consumed by the motion, so much so that she began to hurt herself and

Daniel S. Mishkin, M.D.

had to be restrained. She was demanding, "Get away! Get away! Get away!" as she tried to move her arms. She was obviously talking to something other than the people in the room. When I think about it, the hair on the back of my neck stands up because she passed away a few minutes later.

After countless decisions we think we have control over, we all come to the same end. Every step along the way contributes to the final moment's emotional tenor. No one knows what comes after death. Each person has his own personal belief that shapes his ideas about dying. Some feel sure there's nothing beyond this life. Personally, I believe in God and I think there is some kind of afterlife. Regardless of what any of us believes, it's impossible to prove anything. I can't invoke any kind of Divine knowledge to comfort my patients; to claim to do so would be hubris.

To comfort the dying, I rely on the communication methods I've learned and continue to learn over many years of experience. Dying is a long game: you have to focus on sustaining the patient and their family throughout the process.

Once, I was treating a man in the emergency room, for an acute issue. He'd had lymphoma, but he had been in remission for nearly five years. He felt so close to that five-year-remission milestone, at which we call a cancer patient "cured." That anniversary is a real landmark. I could tell that he was anxious that his cancer had returned. He kept saying "I'm almost there. I'm almost there." He was fixated on a goal that might never come to pass.

Based on the patient's symptoms and initial examination, it was clear that something was wrong. I couldn't be sure it was a relapse, but because of his history, I wanted to help him prepare for the possibility.

I asked him, "What would you do if the cancer came back?"

He replied, "We can't talk about that."

He was in such denial that he couldn't entertain the possibility that his cancer was back. At the same time, he had come to the emergency room due to a health crisis. There were symptoms he couldn't ignore, and sooner or later, he would have to deal with their cause. His avoidance made me uneasy.

I said, "We've got to figure this out." I told him that I thought his acute issue could be related to the cancer and reasked him what he would do if he got sick again. Did he want me to get in touch with his oncologist? What options did he want to explore?

Part of me didn't want to burst his bubble. The other part of me knew that I could help him deal with whatever was happening. It was a difficult situation. I didn't have any kind of tests or proof at that time. I wouldn't be the one to tell him his remission was over; all I could do was care for him along the way. I had to respect his wishes.

The clearest case I've seen for the value of listening to patients came in my second year of medical school, when I was rotating through Introduction to Clinical Medicine. In that rotation, trainees learn to take a patient's history. You practice doing physical exams, but most of the process is about developing patient interview skills. I've never spent as long with individual patients as I did in that rotation. The patients who participate offer up long periods of their time—sometimes hours—so that a medical student can train.

Often the patients who agree to this process are retired, and they feel like they're doing a service to the next generation by participating. But one day, I was assigned a man in his twenties who complained of diarrhea and abdominal pain. He had a new diagnosis of Crohn's disease, and he had been pretty sick. He'd received a colonoscopy and IV medications, and he was on the mend.

In the interview, he and I went through the sequence of events that had brought him into the hospital. I probably asked him a hundred questions in the course of two hours. By the end, we'd become pretty comfortable with each other. Finally, I felt like I was finished.

I asked him, "Is there anything else you think might be important?"

"Well, I'm not sure," he said.

"What do you mean?" I asked.

"Well, there's something, but I'm kind of embarrassed about it. I don't know if I want to tell you," he said.

"OK," I responded. I was curious, but I didn't want to push it. I told him I could come back later and we could talk again.

Then he changed his mind. He told me what had happened.

This patient was a mechanic at the Montreal airport. A couple of days before he was admitted, he was opening an aircraft's hatch to empty the lavatory contents. When he unlatched the compartment, he discovered that the containment system wasn't well sealed. As soon as he opened the door, the entire contents of the plane's toilets emptied onto him. He was covered from head to toe in other people's waste. It was like something out of a slapstick comedy—but I couldn't laugh. I was the doctor; I had to keep a straight face.

Clinically, the information was actually quite relevant. Crohn's disease is a genetic autoimmune disorder, not an infectious disease caused by an outside contaminant, but it can be triggered by environmental factors such as an infectious precipitant. There's a case to be made that the patient's symptoms were precipitated by this exposure. In this case, the fact might be relevant, but knowing it did not change the treatment plan or his overall care. However, if I hadn't spent two hours with the patient, I never would've known.

8
AN IMMENSE EMOTIONAL TOLL

We knew it would take time to find Barry a bone marrow match and get prepared for the transplant process. Would it be weeks or months? We had no idea. Again and again, we saw that if he were going to beat this, it would require an uphill battle.

While it had appeared that we were going down that road over the previous few months, we came to a point when we knew without a doubt that Barry needed a bone marrow transplant, and he needed one quickly. It was February of 2002, nearly three years after Barry's diagnosis. We needed to use our last option.

That January, Stef and I got engaged. By the time Barry was readmitted, we hadn't set a wedding date yet, but we were talking about getting married in October, on Columbus Day, which coincides with Canadian Thanksgiving.

We had thought Barry was doing OK. Once we got the news that his repeat bone marrow biopsy showed progression occurring more quickly than anticipated, our plans were thrown into chaos. I had to have my

Daniel S. Mishkin, M.D.

brother at my wedding. Barry and I were inseparable, and I wanted my wedding to be a chance for him to celebrate his life too. It wouldn't be the same without him. I didn't know what to do. Stef was amazing; she was ready and willing for whatever I wanted to do. I couldn't imagine a more caring or compassionate fiancée. We called our rabbi, who would be our officiant. He suggested moving the wedding up to March. We liked that idea and decided to go ahead with it. Looking back, I know that he was right, as usual.

With the wedding now scheduled for March, we had just four weeks to plan this major event. Everything was last minute; we created the invitations in a day, with the RSVP directed to the home phone number of my sister, Sharon. Sharon was on top of everything. She was there for Stef emotionally and logistically when I had to be at work, and even in another city. She took on as much as she could, without being asked. That's who she is to this day. Sharon has always been there for me and our family.

We booked the venue for a Thursday night because the Sunday was taken. Stef took it all in stride, with grace, and selfless tact. She worked so hard to improve the odds of Barry's being there, but there was still no guarantee.

That January and February were very hard; Barry was so sick. First, he wasn't responding to treatment, then he was back in the hospital with an infection in his brain. He was having antibiotics administered into the Ommaya reservoir in his brain in an attempt to avoid having to remove the reservoir.

There were further infections, complications on top of complications. Fortunately, he improved just in time to be discharged, continuing on IV antibiotics, so he could make it to his son's third birthday party.

Unfortunately, Barry was readmitted in the middle of February when he developed *Clostridium difficile*, an infection of the colon in which some bad bacteria overtakes the normal, good bacteria and wreaks havoc. It's common in hospital settings, and it can be very dangerous for someone with a weakened immune system. Often, it's a result of the use of antibiotics to fight off another infection. When antibiotics come in and wipe out the normal bacteria in the gut, the *Clostridium difficile* has a chance to strike. These are two separate issues that were occurring simultaneously and weakening Barry's status.

Three days into his treatment with metronidazole for this infection, he wasn't tolerating it well. He was uncomfortable and just miserable. He seemed to be getting worse. I decided to speak to the attending who was taking care of him. This wasn't Barry's primary physician, but another attending caring for him while Dr. V. was away.

"I'm a first-year GI fellow," I explained. My brother doesn't seem to be tolerating this treatment very well. When patients aren't tolerating this drug, we usually switch to vancomycin orally."

The attending nodded.

"You know, that's a great idea. Let's do it."

I was glad that he was on board with the alternative course, but I wanted to make sure he didn't feel like I was pressuring him. Based on my previous experiences, I treaded softly, in fear of resistance.

I asked him, "Why don't you speak to Infectious Diseases and see what they think?"

He agreed. After the consult, he switched Barry to the oral vancomycin. Thankfully, it didn't take long for this to work, and it is much easier to tolerate. Barry was significantly more comfortable, and the infection started to become under control. This improvement was crucial, as we were only two weeks away from the wedding.

Daniel S. Mishkin, M.D.

A couple of days later, Dr. V. returned. He had been wonderful to work with up until this point. He'd been transparent in his communication and realistic in his prognosis. He'd helped with the transfer from Montefiore and the research that led us to the stronger course of chemo. But even the best doctor-patient relationships get tested over time. All of a sudden, something was different between us. It seemed that I'd stepped on his toes. He went into Barry's room and lectured him. I wasn't there, so I'm not sure exactly what he said, but he was angry. He told Barry that I, as a GI fellow, couldn't understand the intricacies of my brother's situation. He told him that my advice could have triggered vancomycin-resistant bacteria, and if Barry ended up in transplant with that resistant strain, he would be toast.

Then, at the end of his tirade, Dr. V. told Barry that, due to his clinical situation, he probably wouldn't be able to attend my wedding, which was just a couple of weeks away. Dr. V. probably hadn't meant that statement to sound vindictive, but Barry took it as a threat and a punishment. That sent Barry into an emotional tailspin. He went back to the moment when the nurse had told him he couldn't shower, when he'd lost control over his own body. Here he was again, with no autonomy. Again, he was being told what he couldn't do, by a judge who seemed skewed, when the decision had actually been made by the primary and infectious diseases teams.

For the whole week leading up to the wedding, we didn't know if Barry would be allowed to come. There was a certain platelet count that Barry had to reach before he would be allowed to travel. We talked briefly about moving the wedding to New York, but if we did that, many other important people in our lives wouldn't be able to come. It would have been tough, but our lives were already crazy.

When emotions are running high, a simple disagreement can become a huge ordeal. This whole time, it felt to Barry and me like Dr. V. was making a power play. After I had made a suggestion that went against what Dr. V. might have chosen to do, the doctor appeared to be wresting control back from the "meddlesome brother." Even if a physician is stating his expert opinion, patients and their families can be exceptionally vulnerable and can take every word and event personally. I know I did.

Barry had missed our sister Sharon's wedding because his immune system had been too weak. He'd recorded a video that we played at the reception. It was funny and sweet, but so sad. The simple home video was courageous and touching, but so heartrending. Everyone had been spellbound. He couldn't bear the thought of missing my wedding too.

Finally, on the Tuesday before my wedding, Barry got the go-ahead. Maybe Dr. V. hadn't meant anything malicious by his earlier pronouncement, but it had made Barry so upset. When the doctor finally spoke to my brother, he said that in the prior instance, he'd had a bad day. Dr. V. used terms of endearment to suggest that he loved Barry and was only looking out for him. While we all have bad days, that one had ended up resulting in someone else having a worse one.

In the end, Barry came to my wedding. He stood beside me as my best man. It wasn't easy, physically, for him to be there, but it meant the world to me. While delivering his speech at the reception, he choked up as he wished us a lifetime of happiness and health. He knew firsthand that wish was easier said than done, making it even more powerful. He stood there with a full head of hair, looking amazing in his matching tuxedo and vest. When he delivered that speech, there wasn't a dry eye in the crowd.

9
A DELICATE BALANCE
Why We'll Never Get It All Right

Stef and I were married on March 7, 2002. At the time, we were so focused on nailing down all the wedding details and getting Barry to Montreal that it never crossed our minds to plan a honeymoon. Little did we know, my brother and sister were planning a huge surprise for us: a trip to Disney World. Barry and Sharon booked our travel arrangements, and they took care of the logistics to get me off work for a week. We got married on a Thursday, drove back down to New York that Sunday, and flew out that Monday. For five whole days, there we were—just the two of us. I couldn't believe that, after doing so much work organizing our wedding, Sharon had gone ahead and taken care of all the honeymoon details. She had allowed me to focus on other things, but she'd also addressed things I never would have thought of. This was crucial, as it was essential for my mental health to be able to continue moving forward. Once again, she was there to save the day.

Daniel S. Mishkin, M.D.

That week at Disney World was a blessing, to be away together for a few days. We realized that our world had been totally consumed with everything else that was going on. When I lived in Montreal, Stef and I saw each other every day. Once I moved to New York for my fellowship, we still made it work with her visits every other weekend. When Barry got sick again, my life went into a tailspin. I was already working, studying for my certification exam and spending time with Stef and my brother and his family. Then there were the bone marrow drives and the fundraising efforts, not to mention hospital coverage and trying to keep up in the specialty training I had just started. I was constantly running from place to place, trying to fit everything in.

That week on our honeymoon, I didn't have anywhere else I had to be. I was in the moment, only focused on celebrating with my new wife. To this day, I cherish that gift.

It's always difficult to go back to the day-to-day after a vacation, but the return from that trip was especially hard. I wasn't only returning to work; I was returning to my brother, who was fighting for his life. There was little more I could do. On a positive note, though, I was so excited to begin my married life with Stef. Now I had a full-time partner to help me through my tough days, and I knew that difficult times were ahead. My brother's way forward was clear: he would have to get a bone marrow transplant. He was already meeting with the transplant hematologist and his new team of doctors. He was going in for the initial tests that would begin the transplant process. That would either put the whole cancer ordeal behind him or it could lead us into real trouble.

The first step was to find Barry a match. In a bone marrow transplant, there are ten antigens that need to be matched between donor and recipient. A match of ten out of ten is the ideal—the closer the two people's genetic markers, the more likely it is that the transplant will not be rejected by the recipient's immune system.

There is an international database of bone marrow donors. This was the database we were helping recruit donors for with bone marrow registration drives. These people had voluntarily joined, choosing to get tested and possibly be called upon to save another person's life. We knew that most of the people we'd recruited wouldn't be in the database yet, though, because it takes time to process samples and enter them into the system.

When they ran the database, they found a match for Barry: a nine out of ten. It wasn't perfect, but it was close. At the time, the thought was that fewer than nine common antigens posed a problem, but a match of nine was fine. Ten would have been better, but that just wasn't available.

After the wedding, Barry went into intensive transplant preparation. At that time, he was formally transferred from the care of Dr. V. to the transplant team, who specialized in the delicate work ahead. The transfer was difficult for Barry. Despite the ups and downs with Dr. V., Barry trusted him. We all did. The transplant team was great. They were friendly and helpful, but we only met them when Barry was placed in their care. Barry was a doctor; he knew that the new team had access to Dr. V.'s notes and could consult with him. Still, it was tough. Perhaps it was the instability inherent in every aspect of his health at that point in his treatment, but I always perceived that Barry felt a bit abandoned. He went from a team that knew him well to a completely unfamiliar team. In terms of building relationships, he had to start all over again. Unfortunately, there just wasn't time for any of that. The transplant process had to get under way.

This transplant was the last ace up our sleeve; for the previous two years, we had known that if the chemo did not work, we could always turn to a bone marrow transplant. Now, this was the card we had to play. We held nothing in reserve.

Daniel S. Mishkin, M.D.

Barry's medical team calibrated everything so that his body would be primed for receiving the donated cells. A reciprocal process was taking place for the donor. Earlier in the history of the procedure, the bone marrow donation process was a much riskier and more difficult ordeal for the person voluntarily deciding to help a cancer patient in need, the donor. Doctors would drill dozens of holes directly into a donor's hip bones and harvest the marrow directly. The donor would then require weeks of bed rest to recover. By the time my brother needed the transplant, the process had become much less involved. Instead of drilling into the donor's bones and harvesting the cells directly, doctors could perform a peripheral collection, the same method that's used now. The way it works is, the donor takes medications that boost the production of bone marrow so much that it seeps out of the bones and into the bloodstream. After ten days of taking bone marrow boosters, the patient is hooked up to two large IVs to filter out the cells. It's a delicate process, but it's considered relatively straightforward, with only some mild bone discomfort on the donor's side.

As doctors, we often imagine that we have control over a patient or a medical situation. We think, *If I only do the right things, know how to make the right decisions, everything will be OK.* What I've learned through my training and my brother's illness is that no human can play God. No doctor can predict all the possible outcomes and prevent every mistake. By the same principle, no single person can take all the credit for saving a patient's life. Just when everything seems to be going according to plan, it can all fall apart in an instant. Mistakes are everywhere. They happen all the time; the best we can hope for is that the mistakes are small and reversible. From the earliest days of my training to the present day, I've been terrified that there's something I'll miss or something I'll do wrong. Most of the time, I see common maladies that a medical student can diagnose, but my experience has taught me to maintain that fear of the rare disease or condition.

As a patient, small delays or moments of confusion can be extremely distressing. Sometimes, the complications of medical treatment don't even have to do with the disease itself, but with the treatment. A number of years back, shortly after we'd had our third child in 2008, my wife started feeling out of sorts. She was getting winded all of a sudden. She couldn't get through her daily four or five miles on the treadmill. So I checked her oxygen level; it was 91 percent.

That's when I rang the alarm. We went to the hospital, where I called her doctor, and we decided to perform some urgent testing. We ran a cardiac echo to make sure it wasn't her heart; then once that was clear, we ran X-rays. Nothing. Finally, we did a CT scan to look for a pulmonary embolism. As Stef was coming out of the scanner, I got a glimpse of her results. It looked like there was an embolism *and* her lung was in danger. I knew that something here did not add up.

For the most part, Stef was—and still is—a healthy young woman; in this case, it was simply bad luck that this issue was accelerating at an unbelievably fast pace. She also happened to be a patient who had experienced intolerances to medications. In many situations, the medicines had done more harm than the conditions themselves.

At that point, I jumped into action.

I kissed Stef and told her, "I'll meet you in the emergency room in ten minutes."

For Stef, that's when it all went awry. She was taken to the emergency room, while I went to consult with a radiologist friend and colleague. She was alone, and she had no idea what was happening.

Daniel S. Mishkin, M.D.

The radiologist informed me that he saw three wedge-shaped infarcts, three areas of restricted blood flow to Stef's lungs. This was exceedingly rare; there had to be something else going on. The radiologists suggested that the problem might be clots, a more common diagnosis. It was possible, but it wasn't adding up. I called a pulmonologist friend. He thought I was grasping at straws, but he was willing to help and came downstairs. I would've done the same if his spouse were in trouble. The three of us started going back and forth, reviewing Stef's chart and bouncing ideas off each other. We narrowed it down to bronchiolitis obliterans organizing pneumonia (BOOP) and eosinophilic pneumonia, both of which are extremely uncommon diagnoses.

The diagnosis took an hour. To Stef, this felt like a lifetime. Her mind went into full panic mode. She kept imagining how bad it might be: Did she have cancer? Was she dying? Someone came in and told her he was about to start her on blood thinners, then changed his mind. While I was chasing down answers with my colleagues, she was calling her parents in a panic. She was calling me, and I wasn't answering because there was no cell reception in that area of the hospital. I was trying to protect her. The hour that it had all taken had felt like five minutes to me, and like an eternity for Stef. I was wrong in leaving her hanging for as long as I did. As a result of this experience, I'm cognizant to try not to do this to my patients who also want instantaneous results. When you're scared, it helps to know what's going on.

In the end, we determined that it was most likely drug-induced BOOP resulting from a medication Stef had been taking. It was a diagnosis I have still never seen in anyone else. Because we'd kept our list of possible explanations open, we had been able to reach this diagnosis. The thing is, if we had just looked at the initial review of the CT, the radiologists would

The Other Side of the Bed

have been justified in diagnosing pulmonary embolisms. But because I knew her entire medication history and we were able to put this scan in context with the whole patient, we got to the root of the problem and avoided giving her the wrong treatment. In the end, the medication-related side effect was reversible. After going on steroids, she got better. I've still never seen anything like this. It looked like a horse and sounded like a horse, but it was a zebra.

How can you look at a situation through objective eyes? You have to keep an open mind to keep from missing critical details. There's a selective-attention test created by Christopher Chabris and Daniel Simons, commonly known as "The Invisible Gorilla." In it, the introductory titles instruct you to "count how many times the players in white pass the basketball." The video proceeds to show six people, half in white and half in black, passing a basketball around and through each other's winding steps. If viewers do as the titles instruct, and focus their attention on counting, almost everyone misses the person in a gorilla suit walking through the frame, which, in retrospect, is very obvious. By looking for one thing, you can completely miss something else—no matter how strange it might be. Often, we see only what we're looking for.

Of course, the question "What's going on?" can be terrifying, and its answer seems different from each individual's own perspective. At one point in 2002, Barry was very sick, in the ICU at the cancer hospital. He was cycling up and down, having a difficult time staying stable. He had just been taken off a ventilator a couple of days before. In this state, he was having altered sleep-wake cycles, and at two in the morning, he was awake. I was there. We were talking.

Then, all of a sudden, in the middle of a conversation, he stopped talking and slumped over. He was in the middle of a sentence, and he didn't finish.

I called out to him, "Barry? Barry? Barry, are you there?"

Nothing. I couldn't wake him. He was hooked up to monitors, but their alarms weren't sounding. His blood pressure, heart rate, and oxygen level were fine.

There are very few symptoms that make a patient go unresponsive so quickly. It has to be due to low blood pressure or oxygen level, abnormal heart rate, some sort of sedative, or low blood sugar. I had seen this before. My guess was that Barry was suffering from low blood sugar, and his body had gone into some sort of shock.

I went out and grabbed a nurse. I told her my brother was unresponsive and asked her to evaluate.

She looked me in the eye and said, "He's probably just tired. It's time for you to go home and get some sleep."

"Look, I'm not going home; he went unconscious in the middle of a sentence! Could you call a doctor?"

Again, she said, "Just let him be; he's tired."

But I wouldn't give in. I found the ICU fellow.

When I told him what had just happened to Barry, he said, "Just let him sleep. I heard from the nurses what's going on. He's just tired. Let him be."

I knew I couldn't convince him of my opinion, but I just wanted him to come make an evaluation on his own. I didn't tell him that I thought he was wrong.

I said, "He's unresponsive. Can you just come and try to wake him up? Do whatever you can?"

The doctor came in and looked at the monitors. Blood pressure, heart rate, and oxygen were still good. Then he rubbed Barry's sternum, a classic way to rouse a patient. Nothing.

At that point, I suggested, "Why don't you check his sugars?"

He shook his head.

"We don't need to. There's no reason to think that he's having a problem with blood sugar."

"I know, but what else could this be?" I asked.

We ended up making a deal: He would check the blood sugar. If his sugar was OK, I would have to leave the ICU for an hour. At that point, I felt a pang of self-doubt. What if I was wrong? I was in the first year of my fellowship; I wasn't finished with my training. I heard one of the nurses call security; they knew that if I had to leave, it wouldn't be without putting up a fight.

Lo and behold, the sugar test came back, and it was dangerously low. They gave Barry sugar in his IV, a bolus of D50, and all of a sudden, he was conscious again, picking up the conversation right where it had been left off. He had no idea an hour had passed. Then he saw the two security guards behind me. I told him what had happened.

Then the ICU fellow cut in.

"You have to leave. I tested the sugar. Now you have to go," he said.

"Wait," I protested. That hadn't been our deal.

The ICU fellow kept trying to insist that it had been, and because he'd tested Barry's blood sugar, I had to leave the room.

I begrudgingly left, as I knew Barry was temporarily OK. Although everyone was hoping I'd go home and sleep, I returned exactly sixty minutes later. Barry started to giggle, as he knew something had happened and was waiting for the details. A short time later, the exact same event occurred and he became unconscious mid-sentence. I called the nurse over, and she checked his sugar. When the sugar test came back, it was even lower than before. At that point, I became infuriated. The ICU staff had been so preoccupied with me that they'd forgotten to order maintenance IV dextrose until they'd fully resolved the situation. We figured out that the

Daniel S. Mishkin, M.D.

cause was when the tubing from the TPN[2] bag with insulin was used to flush in antibiotics quickly, essentially a large amount of insulin, that was in the reused tubing line, all at once.

Just a few months after my wedding, Barry was all set to go for his bone marrow transplant. The donor had been identified, and both he and Barry were undergoing the necessary procedures. But then, one day, we got a call from Barry's doctors. In the second round of testing, the donor's bone marrow was showing some abnormalities. The transplant would have to be put on hold.

At first, we thought that this would be temporary. We hoped that things would continue on as planned. The bone marrow transplant was Barry's last chance.

A short time later, we got the news: the donor had early-stage leukemia. This was absurd! Barry's last chance was obliterated. It felt like we'd walked down a clear path, only to arrive at the edge of a cliff.

What do you do when the bottom falls out? What *can* you do? For Barry's treatment, everything that was in motion had to be paused—yet that was impossible. In a bone marrow transplant, an intricate balance of treatments is required to wipe out a patient's native cells. Then, his immune system had to be suppressed in order to accept someone else's bone marrow. He was on prednisone and a precise dose of chemotherapy had been timed for the transplant. The transplant team had revved up and begun to wipe out Barry's native bone marrow, but there were no other cells to put there. His blood counts were incredibly low. We were running out of time.

We had to find another match. We were desperate, but there were no good options. We already knew that there would be no ten-out-of-ten match.

---

2 Total parenteral nutrition (TPN) is a method of providing nutritional supplements in an IV formulation administered through a vein.

Now there was the added stress of Barry's condition. We were unlikely to find a good donor who could jump in in time, but if the transplant didn't go forward, Barry would surely die. We knew that not everyone on the registry would agree to donate on such short notice. The donation process takes time, and it can require the donor to take time off work or away from family. It's not without risk or inconvenience. It's not something everyone is willing or able to do on the spur of the moment, even if he or she has previously enrolled in the database.

Out of sheer luck, there was one person in the registry, an eight-out-of-ten match, who agreed to donate to my brother. We were apprehensive about a match that was obviously less than ideal medically, but what choice did we have? We were grateful to have a donor at all. The person even sent Barry a small figure of an angel that's supposed to watch the recipient in a time of need. We're Jewish, so it wasn't something we would have purchased ourselves, but I'll admit, we kept it in the room; we'd take all the help we could get! Plus, our keeping it there was a gesture of respect for the generous donor.

The new match went through the testing and was cleared to go ahead as a donor. Even though we were behind schedule and the match was less than perfect, we were hopeful. We had to be; we had no choice.

The donor's bone marrow was harvested in an academic center and transported to New York. When people think of a transplant, they usually think of an organ in a special cooler with a police escort. We imagine it to be transported like the Stanley Cup, which travels with a white-gloved chaperone. We think of a transplant as a process in which the patient is under general anesthesia. That's not how a bone marrow transplant works. A transplant of bone marrow cells just looks like a bag of blood. It's infused in a conscious patient just like IV fluids or medication. Barry's bone marrow had already been essentially removed by chemo, leaving space open for the new, healthier donor cells.

Still, receiving another person's bone marrow is a risky process. At this point in his treatment, Barry was walking a tightrope. If he stayed on, he could survive, but if a gust of wind blew, or if he slipped just a little, he would succumb to his illness.

Before he entered the hospital, before he began the chemo and underwent the transplant, he decided to make a video. I assume that the idea was that this was something his son could remember him by, if it came to that. At the end of the video, Barry says, "Jason, I'll be home soon." I have watched that video again and again, and I hope Jason realizes how much Barry loved him and Sari.

As a result of the unexpected delay, by the time the day of the transplant came, Barry had been in Memorial Sloan Kettering for some time. He was on the launch pad and ready for the main event.

I was at work when the bone marrow transplant began. That is when it all came crashing down. We had no idea at the time that there had already been a complication before the bone marrow had ever reached the hospital. A contamination. A mistake.

10
MY BROTHER'S KEEPER

Facing Death with Dignity: It is Possible

In Barry's case, the mistake that was made was, in all likelihood, entirely preventable. We do our best, but the fact is, things will always go wrong. I hate to think like this, but medicine can be like Murphy's Law: whatever can go wrong, will.

On the physician's side of things, it's important to figure out what went wrong and learn from it. On the patient's side, there's also a desire to hold someone accountable. Physicians need to be correct 100 percent of the time; 99 percent is unacceptable.

I began my medical training in Canada, where civil suits over medical outcomes are rare. In the United States, however, lawsuits are a part of almost every physician's career. We're constantly reminded of the legal repercussions of our clinical actions. We spend as much or more time with charts than patients. We pay yearly premiums for liability insurance. Lawsuit prevention is a part of my everyday medical practice. That's just how it is.

Daniel S. Mishkin, M.D.

The first time I was named in a lawsuit, I found out at the end of my fellowship, but the event had happened two years earlier. One evening, I was on my way out the door when I was called for a consult. Barry was still alive and I was headed to the cancer hospital to see him. I was leaving a bit early that day, so I went down to see the patient in the emergency room. Upon examination, I determined that the patient had a rectal abscess, a pocket of infection just outside the colon. It had to be confirmed, but I knew that the man would require a possible drainage and I recommended calling surgery. The course of action was clear. I recommended that the emergency room physician order a CT scan and call surgery as well as start antibiotics.

The CAT scan came back and confirmed my diagnosis. By then, I had left the hospital; I'd done my job in examining, diagnosing, and recommending a plan of care for the patient. I had communicated with the radiologist and emergency room physician who were involved. The surgeon had not seen the patient yet.

The patient needed to have the pocket of infection drained, but someone in surgery said that there was no abscess. So while I was gone, a surgeon performed the wrong procedure, which ended up rupturing the abscess. The infection spread, and the patient lost a testicle due to Fournier's gangrene.

It was clear from the time stamps in the file that the radiologist had told one of the surgical trainees about the abscess before the procedure. Someone in the surgical line of communication had gotten it wrong, and as a result, the patient suffered.

I found out that I was named in the lawsuit just after Barry died, and it felt like a slap in the face. Here I was, mourning my brother's death, the result of so many mistakes, only to be named in a lawsuit. I was devastated.

I knew that I'd been rushing out late that afternoon, but I'd done the right thing. I had made the right diagnosis and communicated with the emergency room physician who was taking care of the patient. I had not made a mistake, so why was *I* being named?

I was upset, and I went into a panic. I told Stef I wanted to leave medicine.

I said, "That's it; I'm done. I don't want to do this anymore."

I knew that it hadn't been my fault, but I was terrified.

The whole matter took a few years to be settled, but emotionally, it hit me hard and still lingers. Medicine is a team sport. As a physician, if the people around you make a mistake, you can take the fall.

I believe that we have to hold doctors accountable for medical mistakes that are preventable. I also believe that, in equivocal cases, we have to protect doctors. Unless there's a clear deviation from the standard of care, we have to give doctors the chance to do their job: care for patients.

Sometimes, the fear of lawsuits makes doctors timid in patient interactions. If we're trying to cover our tracks, it's hard to empathize. However, this is only increasing the overall cost of care.

The way things are now, lawsuits go on and on. Legal fees mount up, and insurance premiums rise. Many physicians hire medical scribes to be present in consultation rooms with them to make sure everything is documented and billed. Along with the increase in lawsuits, physicians are also experiencing falling insurance reimbursements. So, not only is our workload increasing, but so are the costs—meaning, we earn less for our time.

Decreasing the time physicians spend with each individual patient is the primary way in which medicine is dealing with these changes. We squeeze in more appointments so that we can compensate with volume

Daniel S. Mishkin, M.D.

to address the decreased reimbursements, and on and on. That's one of the reasons why patients can feel rushed through and disconnected from their doctors. The systems at play are forcing the situation. It's not good for the profession.

I don't want to sound like I'm complaining about my work; it's obvious that I love being a physician. Despite the difficulty of taking care of people, I've always felt driven to do it.

I was upset about that lawsuit, but the swell of emotions passed. I honestly wish I could just see patients, advise them, give them what they need, and move on. I wish I didn't have to spend so much time in fear of lawsuits, writing every possible note and trying to play the insurance game. Yet we need good doctors to stay in practice. Personally, I am worried that physicians' discontentment will push them out of the profession and cause the next generation to seek other professions. We have to figure out how to learn from mistakes and deal with them in appropriate, proportional ways.

Barry knew that he was in trouble, but he was focused on fighting. He wouldn't allow himself to give in or even stop to rethink what was happening. How could he? Even after the fiasco with the first donor, he kept saying, "Let's do it. Let's do it. Let's do it."

I wasn't there for the actual transplant. Plenty of other family members wanted to be in the room, and from my understanding, I was sure the whole thing would be anticlimactic. It would take time before we knew if the transplant had worked. So I was away, at work, trying to keep plugging away. Barry understood; he had worked the same job. He was being cared for by so many people that I wasn't worried. I planned to see him later that evening.

Barry's body was as ready as it could have been, so the team went ahead with the transplant. Then suddenly, I got an unexpected call from the cancer hospital. The person on the other end of the phone sounded panicked.

I asked, "What happened? What's going on?"

I don't remember much of what he told me, but apparently, a couple of minutes after the transplant had begun, Barry said he didn't feel well. From there, things quickly spiraled downward. He became groggy, then unresponsive. His blood pressure dropped significantly, and he lost consciousness.

I remember thinking, *What could have gone wrong? This wasn't supposed to be a big deal.* I started to panic. This was supposed to be routine.

They put Barry on antibiotics and began the process of transferring him to the ICU for closer monitoring. It wasn't a code situation, but it was worrisome nonetheless. It took about a couple of hours to complete the transfer. Meanwhile, the transplant bag was tested to try to determine if it had been the source of the problem.

As Barry lay in the ICU, his fate unknown, we pressed for answers. Shortly after the ordeal, we found out that the bag was infected. Somehow, the collection itself had been flawed. Even though it had taken place at an academic center—a world-renowned facility—something had gone entirely wrong. This was really bad luck. The transplant that reached my brother was most likely no good, given the contamination in the bag. From the moment the donor cells entered Barry's body, they spread an infection that he had no ability to fight.

After a few days of monitoring in the ICU, Barry was transferred to the main hematology floor. His condition was stable. Now we needed to watch and see if the bone marrow cells survived and were able to establish themselves in Barry's body. I started to fixate on the minutiae of Barry's ups and downs. Every day, the whole family waited for his blood counts to come back from the lab, dreading any new crises. With each new report, the same questions cycled through my head: *Does he need a transfusion? Does he need platelets? Are the*

Daniel S. Mishkin, M.D.

antibiotics working? Is he producing enough factors to coagulate his blood? Day in and day out, we were doing everything we could to prevent complications. Every transfusion holds the risk of infection or rejection, and we had no idea whether the transplant even had a chance to be successful, given the contamination.

When a medical treatment plan goes well, patients don't think twice about the physician and the medical team. However, when complications arise, it's human nature to begin feeling uncomfortable with the medical team. This is especially true if a patient doesn't have a long history of working with the doctor beforehand. The truth is, I think Barry felt a bit abandoned by Dr. V. No one had done anything wrong, but the whole thing could have been handled better. To the best of my knowledge, during all of the complications, Dr. V. never came to visit my brother. In fact, Barry told me that he saw Dr. V. glance into the room as he walked by, yet he didn't stop in. Of course, I can be accused of doing the same thing. There are times I have not gone into a familiar patient's room because I did not know he or she was in the hospital, or there were no active GI problems, or I was just too busy. Thinking about this more, I hope I can start to pay more attention to those relationships. It's a hard lesson for me because I know how upsetting this was for Barry.

As doctors, we try to show empathy to our patients, but we also have to depersonalize their suffering. That's how my brother rationalized Dr. V.'s behavior: Barry's health was failing, and Dr. V. was most likely trying to keep his distance. We can't do our jobs if we're feeling our patients' pain all the time.

Patients can't always see what's going on with their doctors. Even doctors watching each other can't always tell. In a hospital, it's easy for visitors to look around and get frustrated with what they see. Once, my grandmother took one of her friends to the emergency room in Montreal. She came back livid. While she was waiting with her friend, she saw a doctor, in a white coat and all, sitting and reading the newspaper. This was unacceptable to my grandmother. There were patients waiting to be seen, and yet here was this guy sitting around, not even trying to do his job. "There were people waiting!" she said. "All he had to do was call the next patient!"

Or so she thought. Now, my grandmother was a sharp woman. She was rarely wrong. This was one of those rare cases. To her, it looked like the physician was derelict in his duty. After I worked in that emergency room with that exact same physician, though, I saw exactly what was going on: The doctor reading the newspaper was actually supervising a team of trainees. He sat in the middle of the department so that, as his trainees saw patients, they could then easily come and present each case to him. The supervising physician would then, very appropriately, go over and examine each patient himself.

In my view, this was excellent pedagogy. The trainees performed patient examinations that they needed to learn. They were forced to make differential diagnoses on their own before turning to their teacher to be assessed. For doctors, this teaches the evaluation and decision making that are crucial to good patient care. I was truly impressed by the way he ran the department.

Perception is everything. To an outsider, my grandmother, the doctor seemed lazy. To me, he seemed hard at work, doing a great job of leading his team. As a joke, I was always said that in the hospital, it's important to look busy at all times, or someone will give you more work to do. With Barry and Dr. V., we can't know for sure why Dr. V. never came by. As a doctor, there's always a balance to strike between keeping yourself emotionally protected and letting a patient know you care. Maybe Dr. V. knew that Barry was

Daniel S. Mishkin, M.D.

struggling and he needed to distance himself for his own professionalism. I only know my brother felt hurt.

As I continue forward in my medical practice, I try to remember how my brother felt about the small interactions that left lingering emotional effects. These days, I'm lucky to take care of a lot of relatively healthy people. The most common chronic illnesses I treat are liver disease and inflammatory bowel disease; I'm not dealing with prognoses of death on a regular basis like a hematologist or oncologist.

The ill-fated transplant took place in mid-May. By June, Barry hadn't improved much. He was in and out of the ICU from day to day. I was still trying to work. I was shuttling between Montefiore, where I had reduced my workload significantly, and the cancer hospital, only going home to shower. At certain hectic points, I even stopped working. Most nights, my parents were staying in my one-bedroom apartment with Stef—my brand-new wife, who I would only sometimes see in the hospital waiting room. My mom was often attending to everything that needed to be done. She was taking care of Jason so that Sari could be at the hospital, or visiting the hospital so that Sari could be with her son.

I was running on adrenaline, near empty; I wouldn't let myself look past the next day or so. If my mind ever drifted away, toward a future just a few months down the line, I couldn't imagine a scenario in which my brother was still alive. I also couldn't imagine a world in which he was gone.

I don't remember much about this time. We were all doing what we had to, as best we could. My immediate family was supportive, but in reality, we were all too scared to talk frankly about what was happening. My parents were in New York for weeks at a time. We were on edge with Barry's steep ups and downs. Sari was also going through hell, but from a different angle. Barry was clearly in trouble. He was in a downward spiral, getting closer and closer to death.

The Other Side of the Bed

Many years before, my parents had lost a child, a baby. Before I was born, when my brother was five and my sister was four, my mother was pregnant. Very late in her pregnancy, she had a bad contusion to her abdomen. Despite her concerns, her obstetrician didn't feel nervous and thus didn't run any tests. In hindsight, he was wrong.

The baby was born with tremendous, irreparable damage and was immediately taken to the neonatal intensive care unit (NICU). The medical team was appropriately aggressive, as I understand it, but the baby died on its second day of life. The thing is, if this baby had lived, I likely wouldn't have been born; both of my parents have told me that. It's difficult living with that knowledge.

In my second year of medical school, my first rotation happened to be in that very same NICU. I was nervous: rounds were stressful, and I was terrified of making a fool of myself. I was hyperconscious of etiquette: I was told that if someone else senior to me answered a question incorrectly, I shouldn't correct them because that would be insulting. I was as anxious as anyone would be on the first day of work; plus, I had the ghost of a lost baby sibling hanging over me.

I didn't know how to take proper notes, so it was taking me far too long to chart. I kept losing sheets of paper. Early that afternoon, I called my brother to read him my notes in order to make sure that they were medically and legally correct, only to find out that they were entirely wrong. I was in luck, though. Barry was coming to Montreal from New York that night, arriving by plane at eight and coming straight to the hospital. Not only did he help me write perfect notes, he also gave me a big wake-up call by pointing out my incompetence. Documentation is crucial.

Later that night, the resident and I both went to bed. I was awakened at three in the morning, when my pager called me to the NICU. When I arrived, I found a baby who was not doing well. Thankfully, the resident was already there, gathering information. As I watched him stabilize the situation, I felt thankful that I was not the first one to arrive on the scene. If I had been, I would've had to take charge. Did I know what to do? Could I handle it?

Just then, we were called to an obstetrical case room where a woman was having trouble in delivery. We managed the first baby until a nurse ran in, screaming that the newborn baby was not breathing. The resident told me to stay and ran into the other room. I stood there, holding the baby, completely stunned. A skilled nurse saw me look a little flustered and came over to lend a hand and help coach me. It was so much to take in, but I just had to keep moving.

Before morning rounds, I went back to the call room to brush my teeth and wash up. As soon as I was alone, I started to cry. I had witnessed three close calls in the space of ninety minutes. I also realized that, some twenty years earlier in the same room, my family was the one hoping that the young person in the lab coat could save their child. They were the ones to experience that profound loss.

During the long summer of 2002, I leaned on Stef. My family was going through so much emotional turmoil, and Stef did what she could in a difficult situation. She took care of us. She and my mom made sure we ate. She listened to my fears. When I thought I couldn't take it any more, she kept me going. I knew she was incredible when I married her, but she continued to amaze me with her positivity and strength. I'll always be so grateful for that; I still thank her to this day. I don't know what I would have done without her. We all needed each other.

I certainly couldn't have spent much time caring for my brother if his illness had come later in life, after I'd had kids. At the time, I was barely married and still childless. I was in a grueling fellowship program, but my program director was sympathetic to my family situation.

The Other Side of the Bed

Exhaustion was wearing away at the whole family's nerves. We were lucky, though, to be in the company of other families who were dealing with similar circumstances. In the ICU waiting room, we convened with other patients' loved ones and shared experiences with which very few people outside that room could relate. We could say, "I'm worried about so-and-so's platelet count," and the other person would understand. We could tell each other, "That nurse is terrible," or "This nurse is really helpful and gave us the right information." We could mention a complication that occurred in the last round of chemo, and we wouldn't have to explain the whole course the way we might outside that room.

At first, in addition to my family, there was another large, involved family. We had been sitting in this ICU waiting room for days, bemoaning a squeaky hinge: every time the electric door between the ICU's waiting room and patient rooms opened, a screech would pierce through the room. On top of our already frazzled nerves, it was so grating! Every time someone came in or out, we'd wince and moan.

A day or so later, an Italian family arrived: another large ethnic family who were lovely and added to our ICU waiting room team. After just one day hearing this painfully squeaky door, one of the men in the Italian family brought in a can of WD-40. A couple of sprays into the hinge, and *poof!* The sound stopped! The whole ordeal became a running joke, something to laugh about to pass the time. We relied on each other for camaraderie and small acts of generosity that kept our spirits up.

To doctors, relationships between families might seem like a very small piece in the marathon of cancer treatment. But for my family, the relationships we forged injected some extra hope into our days. We could laugh with these people one minute and cry with them the next. It became like a summer camp atmosphere, with unspoken language and inside jokes to bind us. Yet each person's loss took a piece of hope from the rest of us.

Daniel S. Mishkin, M.D.

It was like the movie *Groundhog Day:* the sun would go down and come up, but the day would repeat, over and over, again and again. How were his platelets? What was his white count? Did he need a transfusion? Could he handle a transfusion?

We had a big scare midsummer when Barry got pneumonia. He was in the ICU. I had decided to spend a rare night at home, as I was exhausted. Then I got a call at two in the morning.

"You've got to get over here; Barry can't breathe," said the doctor on the other end of the line.

I arrived in the ICU to find him having a hard time breathing, as if he was choking. He was awake and flailing. While I am sure they were trying to help, I remember feeling as if no one was doing anything for him and that the doctors were just standing there. By the time I arrived, he had been struggling for at least fifteen minutes.

One resident said, "I don't think we should intubate. We should just let him go."

I looked down at my brother. He was looking at me, desperately gasping for air. He looked like he was drowning. But I knew that this wasn't the end for him. He had been OK earlier that day; he probably just had something stuck in his airway. He must have had a mucous plug.

I was livid. He was still conscious! I had to do something.

"Barry!" I said.

When I called his name, he nodded and made eye contact with me.

I went into autopilot. I looked at the doctors and told them what I needed.

"Give me the snake! Get me suction," I said.

I ran a catheter through his nose and used the suction to dislodge what was stuck: a big chunk of mucus. As soon as I removed it, Barry gasped; it was like I had uncorked a bottle. Immediately, his airway was clear. All I had to do was look back at them to know they were embarrassed.

I couldn't believe that they had just stood there when my brother needed something so simple to be done. If I hadn't come in, they would've let him die right then. He was so frail. It was just a matter of time before something would push him over the edge. Somehow, he lived another day.

It's so hard to tell the people you love what you want them to do when you are on your deathbed. What family member is truly ready to say, "It's time to pull the plug"? These situations are ripe for family drama. I've seen terrible conflicts occur when a patient is unable to express his or her wishes. Everyone has his or her own opinion. Often, family members will tell doctors, "Do whatever it takes," to keep their loved one alive. That makes sense if we're dealing with a healthy twenty-five-year-old who's been in a terrible accident. But is that the right course of action for an elderly person with a chronic illness?

I can't advocate enough for living wills. My wife and I have them. A living will is a legal document that details your desires for the end of your life. The document has to name a health-care proxy. It's a person who will make decisions for you if you're incapacitated. It's not enough to simply put your wishes in writing; you have to talk with your health-care proxy and make sure that person knows exactly what you want in various end-of-life situations. So you have to make sure your desires are clear. You have to confront the possibility of death in a frank conversation. Ideally, it's a conversation that continues over time. Toward the end, a patient's desires might change.

I don't want to be a burden on my family, but I know that it would be so difficult to be the one making a decision not to continue lifesaving measures. A health-care proxy needs to feel confident that he or she is carrying out the patient's wishes.

Daniel S. Mishkin, M.D.

I had my first conversation about my end-of-life wishes with my lawyer when my wife and I were drawing up our living wills. When she asked me, "What do you want your advance directives to look like?" the question felt so out of place. She had various suggestions. I imagine they were based on legal precedent, but how much did she know about medical care? Why was my lawyer asking me this question, rather than my doctor?

Can a lawyer truly provide the best counsel for someone making an end-of-life decision? Can a lawyer, even a good one, fully describe the extraordinary measures doctors might take to save someone's life? I'm sure lawyers can do their best, but there are questions that they are unlikely to know the answers to. It is ironic that this discussion occurs in such a matter-of-fact way with a lawyer, and yet physicians shy away from it.

For now, it's up to each of us individually to communicate with our loved ones and medical providers. As a physician, I do my best to encourage my patients to talk about their wishes. I don't want families to suffer the agony of making a decision they're unsure about. It's not easy to talk about, but we have to do it. It's part of our quality of care.

In my case, my wife isn't the only one I've talked to about my end-of-life wishes: my parents and sister know too. I don't want to put my loved ones in a situation where a lack of clarity creates unnecessary tension. My hope is that if it comes to that, the decision won't be the difficult part. If the patient's opinion is known, saying good-bye can be just a little less painful and hold less guilt.

A hundred or so days after the bone marrow transplant, Barry was drained of strength, but his mind was still there. It was a slog, but we were lucky to have one good Sunday with him toward the end. As usual, I was at the hospital, and Barry had felt strong enough to sit up with the support of the motorized bed that moves into a chair-like position. Stef, Sari, Barry, and I just sat in his room hanging out together. Everyone was laughing, we were listening to music—it was just a good day. I still remember him trying to dance. That image will never leave my mind. It had been downhill for so long, but he got that one good day toward the end.

In the first week of August, Barry's blood work began to look like he had a very serious complication called graft-versus-host disease (GVHD). Transplant patients are at high risk for it. In this condition, the immune cells in the unfamiliar graft (the bone marrow transplant) fight against the cells in the body of the host (the patient). The donor cells that were introduced to help the patient end up turning against him. There are a number of symptoms that indicate the condition, and Barry had many of them.

If a patient has GVHD, it has to be treated quickly. It can progress very rapidly, so Barry's doctors decided to do a colonoscopy and gastroscopy to evaluate him; a biopsy result would take a few days. The initial biopsy from the procedures showed that it was likely GVHD, so they decided to go ahead with treatment. Based on how everything appeared, it was the right thing to do. They started him on the additional immunosuppressant medication Remicade˚. It would stop the donor cells' immune response and keep them from attacking Barry's native cells. In ninety-nine cases out of a hundred, it would've been the right choice.

A few days later, the biopsy result came back from the lab: Barry had an adenovirus infection, not GVHD. While the initial evaluation was very reasonable, the final interpretation was different than the initial assessment suggested. Instead of suppressing the immune system, the doctors should've been amplifying it. The medication was making him sicker.

It became clear that his bone marrow was never going to recover. The combination of factors was impossible to overcome. First, there was the destruction of Barry's bone marrow prior to the transplant. Then it was the infection that must have damaged the infusion. After that, it was an endless cycle of infections and dangerous blood levels. Now, the Remicade* was the last obstacle for his immune system to confront.

I don't blame the doctors for making the choice they did. They played the odds. Ninety-nine percent of the time, they would've been right.

As a brother, and as a doctor, I understood that decision. I probably would have done the same thing. I was even part of the decision-making team when they presented us with the options. It just so happened that this one percent anomaly was my brother Barry. Barry's immune system was shot. His body was so weak from months in the hospital, unable to move; this infection just happened to be the thing that did him in. It was one tiny missed opportunity at the end of a long string of unfortunate events. Barry had nearly died so many times, but it looked like this complication would be his last.

Unfortunately, I don't know if everyone in the family understood yet. We'd been at this point before, and somehow, each time, Barry had pulled through. We always had hope.

At that point, I took a leave of absence from work—I had to be with my brother. I wouldn't leave the hospital. It was almost like the early days when he first got sick, when we'd stay up watching *The X-Files*, game shows, and reruns of old shows like *Cheers*. We would listen to music, just spending time together while trying to take his mind off what was going on. To this day, when I watch certain shows or hear certain songs, I return to that time. When I hear the song "Beautiful Day" by U2—or glimpse a scene in the many Adam Sandler movies we watched together, like *The Waterboy*—I fall apart inside.

A few days before he died, Barry asked for a piece of paper. He could barely move his hands when he scrawled out "I love you," and passed the

The Other Side of the Bed

precious note to me. His hands were so weak, I could barely read the letters. I took the note, folded it, and put it in my wallet. I keep it close and look at it frequently to remind myself what a real struggle is. Others have heard me say that I don't mind going into the hospital in the middle of the night because it could be worse: I could be the patient. Staying up late or working all night, juggling my family and work—these are not real struggles. I'm not sure I would have the strength to do what Barry did. Even in his darkest times, he was always teaching me something.

On the day we found out the biopsy results, he took a look at me and said, "Go get a haircut."

"What?" I asked. My personal grooming was the furthest thing from my mind, as everyone around me could attest.

"Go. You look like shit. You won't have time soon," he said.

I laughed and did what I was told. It was only in hindsight that I realized what he was getting at. In the Jewish faith, after someone passes away, there is a time period in which you can't get a haircut. He must have had the insight that the mourning period was coming soon.

The next day, Barry's doctors called a family meeting.

Before I left his room for the meeting, Barry said, "Good luck. This is our last shot."

He was right. Our family talked with the doctors about the few options left, but there really wasn't much to say. As I've said before, I like to talk to patients about options, but at this point, there were few, if any, left. Everyone understood that Barry would die within days.

When I got back to my brother's room, I didn't know what I would say.

"Do we need to talk?" he asked me.

"I don't think so. It's not good," I said.

"OK," he said. That was it.

I was grateful that he didn't pummel me with questions, because I don't know what I would've said. It seemed like he had found some peace. As a family, we were trying to do the same.

Barry wasn't in pain, but his reserves were entirely tapped out. He couldn't move his legs much. It was hard to imagine that he was the same person who used to work out all the time, who was in such great shape. He'd become so weak that he was not the same person. In Barry's last hours, he summoned energy from profound depths to comfort his loved ones. He was the one who was dying, but he was concerned about *us*. It's how he always was—thinking about others and stepping in to do more than his fair share.

The chance to say good-bye was a real gift. All of us were there, in his room. I got to tell Barry I loved him one last time. I got to promise him that I'd take care of Jason. In the years that followed, I got to feel confident that I was fulfilling the promises I made him, and I'm positive that he would be so proud of Sari for raising Jason so well.

In the hour before he died, Barry asked that nobody talk.

"I want to die in peace," he joked. Inside our heads, we must have all laughed.

We complied. We were just there to be with him, to show him how much we loved him, so we were willing to do whatever he asked.

I didn't know how hard it would be. It didn't happen quickly. We were all standing there, watching the monitors, watching his chest rise and fall. The same thoughts kept cycling through my head. I thought, *I can't do this,* then, *I'm a doctor, this isn't what I'm supposed to be doing,* then, *Is he breathing?* then, *I can't do this,* over and over again. When he finally passed, I felt hot tears begin to stream down my face. In the three years of his illness he had fought so hard; now he was gone. I felt some sick sense of relief when I stood there, beside his body, and let myself cry. A void inside me opened up. Mitch Albom wrote in *Tuesdays with Morrie,* "When a person dies, the relationship doesn't die. It just changes." I felt Barry still with me, but his voice became a part of me, of my memory. He is still with me, nestled in my memory and my heart.

11
AFTER THE CATASTROPHE
Moving Forward

Years after my brother died, I ran into a doctor who had been a psychiatry trainee at the cancer hospital when Barry was sick.

"I remember you," he said.

He was part of the team that did rounds on the hematology floor. He remembered that the attending would always care for my brother directly; he had a real regard for other members of the medical family. According to what he told me, the doctors regarded me as a little bit of a loose cannon. When they knew that Barry was on the way out, they were really worried about what I would do. They saw me there, night and day, unshaven and disheveled. They were worried about me. They knew I was a doctor, and they worried that I would lash out at the medical staff or others who had done their best to take care of Barry, though there were plenty of times when things didn't go as planned. They saw the similarities between the two of us, and they were concerned that I would completely fall apart after losing a huge part of myself.

Daniel S. Mishkin, M.D.

The psychiatrist also remembered that he and his fellow residents really identified with Barry. Here was a healthy young man, someone in the prime of his life, who just got unlucky.

After my brother died, I was relieved that he was no longer suffering, but I also felt a new burden: Barry's unfinished business. He was thirty-four years old when he passed away. He was so smart, and he'd spent his whole life in school. He'd graduated from high school, college, and medical school. He was a resident, then chief resident, then a GI fellow, but he'd never finished his fellowship. He hadn't completed his training. He'd never practiced on his own. He was proud of all he had achieved, but he felt a deep anxiety about leaving his young family burdened by his debt. He'd dedicated his adult life to medicine; he had gone through all the rigorous training, but he never saw the payoff.

Barry wanted something good to come out of all his suffering. He wanted other doctors to learn from his experience and put more consideration into their patient interactions. He also wanted patients to understand what might be going on in doctors' minds. Both sides deserve a window into the other's experience, and Barry felt that he was the one who could give it.

Barry had begun writing a book before he died, and I wanted to finish what my brother had started. I tried writing it very soon after he passed away, but it was too much for me. I was still so raw and angry. I couldn't handle thinking through everything that had happened. He was so young. I could still feel a wince of pain at the thought of each mistake.

I knew that none of the doctors meant to hurt Barry, but all the small things added up. What's more, I was still working at Montefiore. Barry had worked there since medical school; everyone knew and loved him. Their condolences were well-intentioned, but the constant pity made me even more conscious of my grief. There was also the setting: every corner of the hospital was full of memories. In the course of any day of work, I might walk by the room where Barry and I watched TV shows late into the night during his first two rounds of chemo. There were so many triggers. Everything around me seemed designed to remind me of the unlucky mistakes that accompanied Barry's terrible diagnosis. Even worse, I would be walking through a hallway and see Dr. K.

I was consumed by circling thoughts of *What if?* I was losing sleep and having a hard time at work. One of the GI attendings, a doctor who really loved Barry, had an unbelievable ability to see the forest for the trees. Whether he was seeing patients, running teaching rounds, or looking at the situation Barry was in, he could put the circumstance into perspective better than most. He had always been someone I looked up to as a humble and brilliant physician and teacher. When Barry got very sick around the time of the transplant, I would call him every day to review the events and make sure I was seeing things correctly. He was a great help to me then, and he remained so after Barry died. One day, not long after Barry had passed away, he told me that he was concerned about me. He could see a change in my demeanor, and he was worried. He knew I was grieving and wanted to do whatever he could to help.

"I know someone you can talk to," he told me. He suggested a friend of his, a psychiatrist, who he thought could help me with what I was going through.

Now, I'd never seen a therapist and I'd never considered myself to be someone who would. For goodness sake, I wasn't crazy! Wasn't it normal to be grieving? But when this other doctor made the suggestion, it sounded right to me.

I was hesitant, but others' encouragement helped me to feel better about going to talk to someone. There's a social stigma attached to talking about mental health, not entirely unlike the stigma attached to talking about death. Even a decade later, I've never told more than a handful of people about this.

I'm writing about it because, for me, seeing the psychiatrist really helped. I needed a neutral professional who was experienced in dealing with emotions like the anger that was overwhelming me. With him, I felt comfortable talking about the thoughts that kept running through my head, without fear of judgment. Not only was I dealing with my brother's death, I was also sorting out my feelings of failure.

So much of what I was going through was the natural process of grieving. After three years at my brother's side, fighting for his life, we had lost. I found myself in a situation not unlike the one Barry had experienced just a couple years before, when his friend died. I didn't want to talk about it with my parents, sister, or sister-in-law. They were grieving too. I didn't want to bring them down with me.

Seeing a psychiatrist helped me to gain perspective on all of it. For my grieving process, that's all I could ask for. While it took some time, I also needed time for closure, if possible. Barry will never come back, but the pain of his loss does diminish over time.

The day that my brother died, I just wanted to hide away. My sister was staying in a hotel, so we all went over there. I felt drained. We were calling people to let them know, figuring out the funeral arrangements—doing all the things that you have to do after someone dies.

At one point, we all sat down and tried writing a eulogy. Each one of us took a stab at it—my parents, my sister, and I. I really didn't want to do it. I didn't think I could get through the delivery without breaking down. But no one else would do it. My sister said she couldn't; I knew my parents wouldn't be able to. It fell to me.

If you knew me as a child, you'd think it was ironic that I was the one to give my brother's eulogy. Back then, I was very shy, and I rarely left my

The Other Side of the Bed

parents' side. Later on, in high school, when I was required to participate in a speech competition, I got Barry to help me. He helped me think through the possible topics from a city-wide list, and we ended up coming up with a humorous speech we called "Men Are What Their Mothers Make of Them." There's no doubt, our mother was crucial to my development. This speech helped me to gain the confidence that led me to be the school representative to the city-wide contest. I was even written about in the *Montreal Gazette*. Barry helped me to get over my fear of public speaking. Now, it's second nature. I'm constantly giving presentations, with and without preparation. In the end, it felt fitting that I would be the one to speak about Barry at his funeral.

After the eulogy was decided, Stef and I went home to get a little bit of a break. Then I started writing. Even though it was a funeral, I didn't want it to be a sob story. I wanted to celebrate my brother's life. It did not take long, thinking back on all the stories, to come to what I would talk about. It was important to remember him for the person he was, not who he became with the illness. Given my exhaustion, I fell asleep and woke up at three o'clock in the morning to write the eulogy. I thought back on the past couple of years, throughout the time when we were in the fellowship program together. Pretty quickly, I knew what stories I'd tell. I would tell stories that I hold dear when I look back on our lives. He taught me to live each day to the fullest, giving everything to those around me. We never know what day will be our last.

One of the stories I recounted in Barry's eulogy began on a normal day, just like any other. We were both working as GI fellows at Montefiore. On Monday mornings, all the GI fellows would meet up for teaching conference, led by the chief of the division. Now, the chief of gastroenterology was a stickler for dress code. He wore a bow tie most days, and if you were on his

Daniel S. Mishkin, M.D.

service, you had to dress to impress. Every man who worked for him had to wear a tie. If your shirt and tie didn't match, you'd get singled out and picked on; God help you if you showed up to conference without a tie.

One day, I showed up to conference just in time for it to start and saw my brother across the room.

I heard him yell, "No, no, no, no!"

Then everyone else started laughing. I looked down and realized why: Barry and I were wearing the same tie. Our parents had given us both the same tie, and we'd worn them on the same day. What's more, we were wearing the same khaki-style pants and blue dress shirt too.

"Take it off!" Barry cried.

"No way!" I told him. If I wasn't wearing a tie, I'd be in the crosshairs for the whole conference.

"I'm your older brother; show me some respect!" he yelled.

"I'm gonna get killed!" I said.

Just then, I heard the chief of gastroenterology coming through the conference room door. At the last second, I tore off my tie. The chief looked straight at me and scowled. For the next hour, he bombarded me with every possible question.

It was an exhausting session, but when Barry and I walked out the door, we looked at each other and smiled. We laughed and joked about it. It became another bonding experience for my brother and me. I took the heat so that he didn't have to. After that, I started keeping an extra tie around, just in case.

Sometimes, laughter gets you through the worst of times. I was always content playing the fool for Barry. No matter what we did together, I just wanted to be with him. At the funeral, I could barely look up from my printed speech, but I could hear people laughing along and I knew we were remembering him as he'd want us to.

A picture of young Barry. Summer of 1987

Barry and I at the Stanley Cup victory parade for the Montreal Canadiens. June 1993

picture from my medical school duation. Barry flew in for the day post- and surprised the family. May 1998

Barry as the Best Man at my wedding with Jason in the center. March 7th 2002

ACKNOWLEDGMENTS

This book has been fourteen years in the making. I've started it many times, then put it down because it was just too painful. I'm so proud it's finally finished. It has been challenging, gut-wrenching, and mentally exhausting, yet very cathartic and satisfying. I can finally cross it off my bucket list.

This book would never have come to be without the help of my immediate family. Thank you to my parents who put up with my shtick, knowing it was all out of love. To my sister, Sharon, and brother-in-law, Mark: you were a perfect sounding board and, as always, a perfect support. To my wife, Stef, for being my lifeline and best friend—without you I could not get through the day. To my three beautiful girls who bring a smile to my face each day. I'm blessed that you feel like my brother is truly a part of your world thanks to the many stories you've heard about his legacy. Two of you are actually named for Barry, and amazingly, I see many of his incredible traits in all of you. To Sari, Barry's wife: you are both my family and my friend. I know, from the bottom of my heart, that Barry is so proud of you for raising Jason to be such a mensch.

I also want to acknowledge my many mentors who've guided, supported, and paved this phenomenal path for me. I would like to thank the wonderful Riverdale community, and Jay Feinberg, who were so unbelievably thoughtful and generous with acts of kindness and continued support. A few honorable mentions go out to Mike Green for his hospitality, John Reinus for his constant ear during my times of need, April Shamy for always picking up the phone, and Lawrence Brandt for teaching me to be a strong patient advocate—and always being Barry's advocate too.

Finally, I want to thank all of the doctors, nurses, and medical personnel who took care of Barry at various points in his treatment and who, despite some errors, had Barry's best interests at heart. You truly wanted what was right for him.

One of the many attributes that made Barry so unique was his leap-year birthday of February 29. He reached eight birthdays, a fact that exemplified his desire to always remain a kid. To those who knew him outside of the hospital, he was always smiling, had a contagious giggle, and was funny, as well as playful at heart. He was full of life, hope, and potential. He had so much to offer the world. I want to celebrate his many accomplishments. I would never want him to be remembered only by his illness.

Daniel S. Mishkin, M.D.

ABOUT THE AUTHOR

Daniel S. Mishkin, M.D., C.M., grew up in Montreal, graduated from McGill University Medical School, and completed his residency at McGill University Hospital before moving to New York to complete his fellowship at Albert Einstein College of Medicine. A practicing gastroenterologist, Daniel is dedicated to caring for the whole patient and educating the next generation of physicians at Harvard Medical School. He lives in the Boston area with his family.

Learn more about the author's journey at **www.theothersideofthebed.com**.